It's not about the music

It's not about the music

A journey into worship

Dan Lucarini

EP BOOKS

EP BOOKS
Faverdale North, Darlington, DL3 0PH, England

e-mail: sales@epbooks.org

web: http://www.epbooks.org

EP BOOKS USA
P. O. Box 614, Carlisle, PA 17013, USA

e-mail: usasales@epbooks.org

web: http://www.epbooks.us

First published 2010

British Library Cataloguing in Publication Data available

ISBN 13: 978-0-85234-727-0   ISBN 0-85234-727-8

All Scripture quotations, unless otherwise indicated, are taken from the New King James Version. Copyright © 1979, 1980, 1982 by Thomas Nelson, Inc. Used by permission. All rights reserved.

Printed and bound in the USA by Versa Press Inc., East Peoria, IL.

Dedication

'You *must* come for dinner after church!' With that memorable introduction, Judi and I met Willis Metcalfe from England. Soon, God would use him to help us get started on this new and vital journey into worship.

Willis went home to be with the Lord in June 2009. We thank God for his devotion to Jesus Christ, his ministry of promoting Christian literature for missions, and his service to the gospel. The book is dedicated to his memory and life. Were he here today, Willis would be quick to deflect any praise of himself straight on to the Lord. And so it is fitting to conclude this dedication: to *God* be the glory!

Contents

The road to Ripon

Judi and I were traveling through the Yorkshire Dales of northern England on a brief vacation, a break from my business work near London. The date was November 2001 — shortly after the terrible terrorist attacks on America and also at the end of a bad outbreak of foot and mouth disease in England.

Ripon is renowned for its ancient cathedral where for over 1,300 years people have come to worship God. We wanted to attend the cathedral on Sunday to hear the famed boys' choir and experience Anglican worship music. But we did not have lodging for Saturday night. This was our first time to Yorkshire. We knew nothing about the area and where to stay.

Ripon's town square was under construction, making it very difficult for an American driving in England for the first time — and at night — to navigate around the town. The detour forced us off the main street down a narrow lane, where we passed a modest little Baptist church.

Then we drove along Trinity Lane, Coltsgate Hill and North Street, where a right-hand turn sent us back to the town square and then around the detour again in an endless loop. We felt trapped! It was very late in the evening. I was losing hope that we would spend the night in Ripon, and fast giving up on the Anglican music delights waiting for us at the cathedral.

After three more times following the same detour and passing the same little church, Judi finally remarked, 'Maybe the Lord wants us to attend *this* church tomorrow'; to which I replied, 'Well, if the Lord wants us there, he'll find a room for us in Ripon,' and said a quick prayer.

At North Street, this time I turned *left* rather than right. There, within a few hundred yards, was a little guest house with a spare room and a light left on for weary travelers. Thank you, Lord!

On Sunday morning, we walked to the Baptist church and were warmly greeted by the pastor and a deacon. They quickly deduced we were American tourists, and the deacon insisted we *must* join his family for Sunday dinner after church. I told him, 'Thanks, we'll think about it,' but fully intended to pass on the invitation and tour a castle or manor house that afternoon. After all, we had a vacation schedule to keep.

For a couple of Baptists from America, the worship service seemed very plain and simple. The small congregation filed into the chapel, took their seats and sat in prayerful silence. There was none of the boisterous laughter and chatter to which we were accustomed at church services in the USA.

The service began with hymn-singing accompanied by a piano. I was impressed that the congregation sang every word of every verse, no matter how many. The most ardent singing was during a hymn unknown to us: John Newton's 'How Sweet the Name of Jesus Sounds'.

The pastor prayed for his congregation, for the lost souls in Ripon and for revival in the United Kingdom. The sermon was expository, full of the Scriptures, and given with a straightforward and reverent delivery. There was no 'joking around' or attempts at 'cool' cultural references.

At the end of the service, during the quiet time for prayerful reflection, Judi whispered to me that she felt prompted in her spirit to accept the dinner invitation. Faced with Judi's sensitivity to the working of the Holy Spirit and such an insistent invitation from the deacon, how could I refuse?

We drove to a farmhouse on the outskirts of town for the dinner. During the preparation of the meal, the ladies sang hymns in the kitchen. When we sat down for dinner, our host led us in singing a doxology as our prayer.

Praise God from whom all blessings flow,
Praise Him all creatures here below,
Praise Him above, ye heavenly hosts,
Praise Father, Son, and Holy Ghost.
Amen.

I had never heard this sung outside of a church, nor sung as a prayer with heads bowed and eyes closed. This had a profound effect on Judi and me, and we have since adopted the custom at our home in Colorado.

Later we returned to the church for the evening service and traveled back to the farmhouse for a special meeting afterwards. The pastor had recently returned from visiting Russian churches where he served as a representative for an English publisher with a special emphasis on providing Christian literature for the mission field.

Sensitive to his American guests yet needing to speak the truth, the pastor spoke about the problems created in Russian churches by American mission teams who also brought their 'Christian' rock bands and insisted this was how the Russians should model their worship. He related how this greatly offended the Russian Christians.

When he finished, Judi told him that I was a former worship leader who led rock and roll praise bands but had recently stepped down over concerns about mixing rock elements with worship. We understood the American church music problem he spoke about.

He asked me: 'Have you considered writing a book about your experiences leaving the contemporary worship scene?' I thought he was just being polite in that British way. Little did I know what God had in mind.

Within one year of this 'chance' meeting, my first book, titled *Why I left the contemporary Christian music movement: confessions of a former worship leader,* was published. The book became a surprise best-seller, now on its twentieth printing.

God has used the wide distribution of that little book into thousands of local churches to challenge the leaders of the modern worship movement. It has also encouraged countless Christians who could not go along with the philosophy and practices of modern worship, with the emphasis on pop music and entertainment.

Looking back, we praise God for guiding us to the beginning of a journey only he could have arranged. Consider all the 'coincidences' that would have had to occur otherwise:

- We had never been to Ripon or the north of England. I chose the Yorkshire Dales for a romantic getaway because I liked the Internet photos of the classic English countryside. I could just have easily chosen the Cotswolds instead.
- If it were not for the construction detour in the Ripon town square, we would not have found that little Baptist church.
- If we had not accepted the dinner invitation, we would have visited a drafty old castle or manor house instead.
- I had never written a book. I was never a famous musician. The last thing I wanted to do was write a book about worship controversies and get square in the middle of the 'worship wars'.

Prologue

I believe that God worked in a mysterious way to help me get started on this new and vital journey into the heart of worship. The journey and the lessons learned along the way are the theme of this book.

Part I

GPS
(God's Positioning System)

Chapter 1

It's not about the music

I can clearly imagine your reaction to that statement. 'What? I thought this was a book about worship music with a clever title to grab my attention. Are you serious, Dan? Of all people, with your music and worship background, how can you say that? Surely you know that music is the most important offering we can bring to God?'

To make the claim that 'it's not about the music' challenges the belief held by the majority and questions the predominant worship practice in many churches today. If you survey the worship landscape, there should be no doubt left that modern worship is *all* about the music.

At the end of 2009, Christian artists were asked: 'What do you think was the biggest moment in Christian Music during the past ten years?' Joel Purdy, bass player from CCM (Contemporary Christian Music) band Hearts of Saints, spoke for many when he responded: 'It has to be the corporate worship movement. Artists gravitated toward a U2-esque sound built around a true worship song, giving the listener a deeper worship experience.'[1]

---

1   Kim Jones, www.christianmusic.about.com, December 2009.

Louis Giglio, long-time leader of the modern worship movement, recently remarked that his Passion 2010 worship conference was not just 'an event with really cool bands'.[2] But was it really more than the music? He added some Bible teachers and missionaries in an attempt to diversify this signature worship music event, but are we to believe he could attract 21,000 college students without the all-star worship bands and the passionate rock concert experience?

Michael W. Smith, another leader of the modern worship music movement and a famous musician with one of the best-selling worship albums in history, summed up the belief of many Christians today when he boldly declared:

> 'I really believe all this new interest in worship — the people getting interested and *the new music* that's coming out — it's all a great new thing God's doing ...
>
> 'Can you hear it? *It's in the music.* When *music* helps you enter into the presence of God, you know it. It's you and God.'[3]

Do you believe that? Do you think music is the most important aspect of worship?

A mile in their shoes

I once believed that. I agreed with Smith and other modern worship leaders, and spread this around as a contemporary worship leader at local churches. I learned about worship mainly from contemporary Christian musicians — many of whom were also worship leaders at their home churches — and from leaders of the church growth movement.

---

2   Joshua A. Goldberg, www.christianpost.com, January 4, 2010.
3   From an interview published in *Charisma* magazine, 2003 (emphasis added).

They left little doubt that the most important way to worship God was through music, and mainly with contemporary pop styles.

I thought I knew how to worship God in the way he wants to be worshiped, in a manner that would please him. I encouraged others to encounter God through new worship music, and many times felt the mystical sensations that rippled through a large, darkened auditorium as we sang and swayed to the music. I sincerely believed that this must be the spirit of God moving among us.

Mea Culpa

I was sincere — but sincerely wrong. During an in-depth word study on 'worship' in the Bible, I noticed that music was rarely mentioned in the same context and began to suspect that we were on the wrong road. We were in danger of missing the very thing we claimed to have found in modern worship — the 'heart' of worship itself.

Shortly after that first Bible study on worship, I resigned my post as worship leader in an evangelical church closely aligned with the Purpose-Driven Church. The story of why I left is told in my first book.

The surprising success of that book led to conversations with over three thousand readers, and to many speaking engagements at music conferences and local churches. This responsibility drove me to study biblical worship and the history of Christian worship even more deeply.

On this journey into worship I soon discovered that, like me when I led worship, most Christians today have no idea what biblical worship is. It is a harsh conclusion, I know. But I have a lot of evidence to back that up. In addition to discussing this in thousands of reader e-mails and in-person interviews over the past eight years, I also gave a quiz to conference attendees titled 'What's your worship IQ?'

The vast majority responded that worship was related to the music at their church. They mentioned the emotions associated with a satisfying musical experience. When asked where they learned about worship, they replied that it was from worship leaders, music ministers, CCM artists and experiences in worship services.

Some respondents showed a broader understanding of worship beyond the music. But this was only in theory, because their actual worship practices showed that music was 'number one' in their hearts. The belief that worship is all about music was not limited to churches with contemporary-style services. I heard this from members of traditional churches too.

The biggest shock of all? My ministry puts me in contact with pastors from around the globe. I discovered that many of them have a thin, surface knowledge of biblical worship topics. As a result they were not equipped to critically evaluate new innovations of modern worship that swept over their churches like a tsunami. They delegated this vital area to the musicians.

Ignorance is not bliss

But is there anything wrong with this lack of knowledge? Yes. We were created to worship our Creator. It is impossible to overstate the importance for *every* Christian to learn as much as possible about the worship of God, and base his or her practices on that, rather than on personal experiences or second-hand information. People can tell a lot about your god from the way you worship him. Getting that *as right as you can* should be beyond dispute. The very honor of God's Holy Name is at stake!

In their ignorance, some church leaders and their followers risk missing the mark and, worse, could fall under the same withering judgement that Jesus directed squarely at the worship leaders of his day:

> And in vain they worship Me, teaching as doctrines the commandments of men.[4]

Would you like to know what worship practices are based on timeless Bible truths, and which ones are the mere 'commandments of men' or contemporary fashions? Are you curious to find out why I think we need to take music off its pedestal?

This book will assume you are a worshiper of God or very interested to learn more about it. We will take a close look at what God has asked us to do in worship and you can compare that to how we worship today. You will not find anything radical in here; just some basic lessons about worshiping God, taken from the Bible and analyzed through the lens of church history.

I am not a university-trained theologian, and I am not a pastor of a church. I am not a musician who has his own worship music to sell you. I no longer lead worship for reasons that will become apparent in this book.

I am a fellow traveler like you, navigating through the landscape of the worship wars and trying to use God's Positioning System — the Bible. I can offer some friendly advice that comes from extensive Bible study, research from thousands of personal contacts, and observations from experience. Call it a 'view from the pew'.

And don't worry — I am not pulling a Zwingli[5] and calling for a ban of all music in church. I simply ask that we consider calling a 'time-out' from our love affair with worship music, step back

---

4   Matthew 15:9. While in the context Jesus was referring to the traditions of the Jews, I believe this warning will apply to anyone who creates 'new traditions and doctrines' for worship that are based on the preferences of men rather than the Word of God.
5   Ulrich Zwingli was a Swiss reformer in the 1500s who banned worship music from his churches.

from that bias, and rebuild our knowledge of worship. Then, properly informed, we can put music back into its right place.

Goals of the book

1. To learn what the Bible teaches about worship and compare that to music-driven worship.
2. To understand the acts of Christian worship that please God the most. You may be surprised to see how that differs from what passes for worship today.
3. To improve our personal and public worship. Worship is not a spectator sport; each Christian must personally be involved.
4. To help us develop a healthy resistance to worldly fashions, fads and styles that are like viruses infecting our personal and public worship.

Knowledge alone can make us proud and arrogant, unless it produces more love for God and more love for our fellow Christians.[6] Therefore I urge you to carefully use this knowledge to:

- Love the Lord your God with all your heart and with all your soul and with all your mind.[7]
- Discern the things that are best, in order to be sincere and blameless until the day of Christ.[8]
- Help fellow Christians who are struggling with this and badly in need of instruction and encouragement.
- Gracefully endure through a bad church experiment with modern worship, without contributing to the malice or slander that often accompanies it.

---

6   1 Corinthians 8:1-3.
7   Deuteronomy 6:5; Matthew 22:37.
8   Philippians 1:10.

Is your church changing, innovating and experimenting with modern worship? You may need an anchor to ride out the storm. Do you fear you may not be in God's will because you cannot support the new worship styles at your church? When you learn more about worship, the fear will go away and Sunday mornings or whenever you meet to worship can become less stressful.

If you are interested to learn more about worshiping God beyond the music; if you're a refugee from the worship wars; or if you're simply curious why someone like me would do an about-face from the accepted norm of modern worship; then please join me now on a journey into the heart of worship.

And discover why 'it's not about the music'.

Chapter 2

The amazing change in worship

How should I worship God?
This question has been debated vigorously since the beginning of Christ's church, and is the source of bitter disputes past and present. If you think our 'worship wars' are terrible, read any history of the Christian church for some perspective. You will quickly discover that most Christians today live in relatively tolerant times, enjoying some degree of freedom to worship without an oppressive state-sponsored church to persecute us.

Today we fight mainly over whether rock and pop music styles are acceptable or not for use in God's service. Some think that is a trivial pursuit. But how can it be trivial, when music has the dominant position of attention in our churches?

We live in a Christian age where music performance is the focal point and given the lion's share of time, energy and praise at most worship services and religious gatherings. No wonder that we fight over it, given the over-sized importance we have assigned to it.

But what if we're missing the point entirely? What if music is not the *main* thing about worship?

What did Jesus say?

Let's consider what Jesus taught us about worshiping God. In John chapter 4, Jesus announced an amazing change in worship.

'But the hour is coming, and now is, when the true worshipers will worship the Father in spirit and truth; for the Father is seeking such to worship Him. God is Spirit, and those who worship Him must worship in spirit and truth.'[1]

Who was he talking to? The Samaritan woman at the well. After Jesus miraculously told her all the details of her private life and marriages, she said, 'Sir, I perceive that You are a prophet.'[2] She decided to bring up the big worship dispute between the Jews and the Samaritans: where is the proper place of worship? She said, 'Our fathers worshiped on this mountain, and you Jews say that in Jerusalem is the place where one ought to worship.'[3]

In Jesus' day, this was a full-blown worship war. The Samaritans built a temple on Mount Gerizim similar to the one in Jerusalem. The Samaritan version of the Pentateuch (the five books of Moses) used the word Gerizim and the patriarchs were thought to have worshiped nearby. They contended Mount Gerizim was the proper place to erect the temple and worship God there.

The Jews on the other hand believed you must worship at the temple in Jerusalem or you were breaking the Law and your worship was in vain. No wonder the Jews and Samaritans despised each other.

The main dispute was over *where* they worshiped. *How* and *when* they worshiped God was similar. Each brought blood-spilt animal sacrifices daily, burned the bodies on the altar, and followed the order of worship according to the Law. Both sides

---

1   John 4:23-24.
2   John 4:19.
3   John 4:20.

were deeply committed to this way of worship because God himself commanded them in the Pentateuch to worship him in this manner.

The shocking claim

Jesus responded to the woman with an astonishing statement that would change for ever the way God is worshiped on earth:

'Woman, believe Me, the hour is coming when you will neither on this mountain, nor in Jerusalem, worship the Father.'[4]

One can understand why Jesus, a Jew, would declare that the Samaritans' worship on Mount Gerizim was wrong. But neither in *Jerusalem*? Who was this man to declare that God's worship would no longer occur in the accepted place?

God himself ordained this system of worship from days of old. After sin entered the world through the fall of Adam and Eve, humans could no longer have a direct relationship with God because of his holiness. God commanded his earliest followers to worship him through sacrifices of animals and food. Abel, Noah and Abraham are among the ancients who worshiped God in this manner.

Pagan worship was a corruption of the original worship to the Creator, the Most High God. They worshiped to appease the angry gods and seek their blessing. The pagan worshiper brought animal sacrifices and food offerings so the gods would not punish them, and to gain favor for crops, wealth, fertility and power.

Then God gave the Law to Moses and it contained very specific instructions on how to worship him. God's people were required to worship as follows:

---

4   John 4:21.

1. *At a specific place* — at the tabernacle and then the temple in Jerusalem. If you were not physically present at the ordained place, you could not sacrifice. But you were required to pray towards the place of worship, twice daily.

2. *At a specific time.* God commanded that morning and evening sacrifices must be offered seven days a week.[5]

3. *With a specific offering.* The worshipers were required to bring special animal or grain offerings to atone for their sins, to keep peace with God, and to show their gratitude to God. These offerings were described in detail in the Law. No freelancing or personal choice were allowed. If you tried to offer any sacrifice that did not conform to the Law, you risked immediate death at God's hands.

Suddenly and without warning, Jesus announced the end of this system of worship. The implications were staggering. This statement must have shocked or dismayed his disciples.

The woman at the well knew enough religion to respond: 'I know that Messiah is coming (who is called Christ). When He comes, He will tell us all things.'[6] Jesus said to her, 'I who speak to you am He.'[7] With that, Jesus established his authority to announce the amazing change in worship.

However, this change must have been very hard for the disciples to accept. They were good Jews who observed the Law and respected the religious and worship customs of the day. This announcement also would have infuriated the religious leaders who presided over the temple worship.

No one understood the impact on Jewish worship better than Jesus. He was a perfect Jew who attended the synagogue on the Sabbath, went to Jerusalem to celebrate Passover, and

---

5   1 Chronicles 16:40.
6   John 4:25.
7   John 4:26.

spent time at the temple. He sang hymns after the Passover meal and read the Torah in public. I think this declaration might have been as controversial as his prophecy that the temple would be torn down stone by stone.

The amazing change in worship

How does this affect us today? Jesus was announcing the end of the worship practices of the Old Covenant, and the beginning of the worship practices for the New Covenant, under which Christians can worship God.

Now at the time Jesus had yet to finish his work on the cross, where he 'offered one sacrifice for sins for ever'[8] and put an end to the daily sacrifices at the temple. It would be another forty years before the temple was destroyed by the Romans, putting a final stop to the old sacrificial system by obliterating the specific place of worship.

But when Jesus announced the change to the woman at the well, the new way to worship God was already standing there — in the person of Jesus the Messiah. His amazing statement implied that:

1. Worshiping God is no longer bound to a specific *place*.
2. Worshiping God is no longer bound to a specific *time*.
3. Worshipers are no longer required to bring specific *material sacrifices* for their sin offerings or peace offerings.
4. Worshipers are no longer required to come to God *through a special priesthood of men.*
5. True worship is from the *spiritual-inner* man, not from the carnal-physical man.
6. God was seeking *new worshipers.* There were no worshipers allowed into the new way of worship based on their Jewish

---

8 Hebrews 10:12.

heritage or their parents' faith. Everyone on planet Earth had to re-apply through Christ for access to God.

This amazing change is incredibly important for all the Gentile readers, because at this moment Jesus opened a new way for people who were not Jews to worship God acceptably.[9] What is that way? Jesus said, 'I am the way, the truth, and the life. No one comes to the Father except through Me.'[10]

The new way is opened to us through the blood of Christ shed for our sins on the cross.[11] Christians can draw near to God through Jesus, who is our great High Priest representing us before God in heaven. We are no longer bound to follow the old worship system — we're free!

What now?

But this amazing change raised immediate questions for Jesus' disciples about how to worship God, questions that still confuse and divide his disciples today.

- How do I worship God?
- Where do I worship God?
- When do I worship God?

At least the old system had very strict rules and regulations, so you knew exactly how or how not to worship God. The old worship system was the epitome of the regulative principle of worship. Nothing was left to the imagination and preferences of men.

But the old system of worship through the tabernacle and temple was done away with and we do not have the option to go

---

9   Hebrews 10:20.
10   John 14:6.
11   Hebrews 10:19.

back to it. The book of Hebrews is one long and stern warning that Christians can never return to the Levitical sacrificial system, no matter how men try to coerce us to do so.

However, humans being humans, we need guidelines and rules to order our behavior. Worship is such an important duty that we do not want to do it in the wrong way. So what replaced the old way to worship?

Every Christian group today will gladly rush into that vacuum and recommend their own rules and regulations and customs. The modern worship music industry and its artists will tell you how to worship. I am a critic of my generation's worship innovations. Sadly, they are only following in the footsteps of a long and regrettable tradition through the ages.

Regardless of where you came from or where you are sitting today, every Christian has a duty to know more about worshiping God. When we are converted, the Bible tells us we are like infants who need milk as our spiritual food.[12] To feed and grow, we rely on the wisdom and knowledge of mature Christians who have experience in handling the Word of God.

But we are all expected to be weaned off the milk and move on to a diet of strong meat for our spiritual food. We find this meat by studying the Scriptures carefully and diligently. This growth process has great benefits for us, one of which is that we become people who 'have their senses exercised to discern both good and evil.'[13]

Summary

Where are you in your worship 'diet'? Still sipping someone else's milk? To those who take their worship knowledge from their church traditions, or from popular contemporary preachers, or

---

12   1 Peter 2:2.
13   Hebrews 5:14.

from modern musicians, I would like to challenge you to try a new diet of strong meat.

At the very least, when we know more about worship it will encourage us right where we are. Or we may come to see that some of the worship practices we are involved in are unnecessary or even unbiblical. Then we will have a good basis to press for change.

I pray all of us will desire to discover how God wants to be worshiped and stop wasting our time in vain worship, practicing the 'commandments of men'.

Chapter 3

Worship by the Word

The meaning of the word 'worship' has changed over the centuries, since it was first widely distributed to English speakers in the 1611 Authorized Version of the Bible (the King James Version). From its original meaning, 'worship' has been greatly expanded by Christians to include many different things.

It can mean a worship service itself, or anything that occurs within the service; for example: dancing; drama; art; fellowship time; music; and so on. Some leaders today even promote a personalized, 'It's between me and God — whatever suits my taste', form of worship.

Such diversity of meaning is the root of many problems. When we do not know what a biblical word means, or when we change its meaning to suit the fashions or felt needs of our contemporary times, either way can lead us to add worship practices that can offend or even divide the body of Christ. Worse, we risk offending the Holy Name of God.

Definitions

Can we find a common meaning that is agreeable to all parties? That's not easy to do. Words are notoriously hard to pin down these days. But since Christians are a 'people of the Word', we should give it a good try.

Let's start with a definition from an English dictionary. According to the *Oxford English Dictionary*, worship means:

1. the feeling or expression of reverence and adoration for a deity;
2. religious rites and ceremonies;
3. great admiration or devotion;
4. His/Your Worship — chiefly British, a title of respect for a magistrate.

The first two meanings are most relevant to our discussion of the worship of God. The first speaks about the individual expression and feeling, while the second relates to the public religious display of that expression. Later we'll take a closer look at the part 'reverence' plays.

Worship combines two Old English words with German origins: worth (to honor) and –ship (to create). The Germans have their own standard word for worship: *Gottesdienst* — literally, 'God-service'.

Where the English say worship, Spanish and French Bible translations use a variation of the word 'adore'. The Old French word is *adourer*, derived from the Latin *adōrāre*, which interestingly means 'to pray to'.

Original languages

The word 'worship' was chosen by English translators to best represent the meaning of the words found in the original Bible languages, Hebrew and Greek. Let's take a look at those original words.

In the Authorized Version of the Old Testament, the word worship and its stems (worshiped, worshiping, worshiper, worshipers) appear in approximately 110 verses.[1] In 99% of those verses, the Hebrew word is *shachah*. *Strong's Concordance* defines *shachah* as 'to depress, to prostrate (especially in homage to royalty or God); to bow oneself down, to crouch, to fall down flat, to humbly beseech'.

Shachah appears in approximately 166 Old Testament verses, and the most common English translation (other than worship) is 'they bowed down their face on the ground'. As you read verse after verse, it becomes clear that the worship acts of Old Testament believers were performed with great respect, fear and reverence towards God, demonstrated by falling down before him.

In the Authorized Version of the New Testament, the word worship and its stems (worshiped, worshiping, worshiper, worshipers) appear in approximately seventy-two verses.[2] There are several Greek words underlying the English translation. We'll start with the most often-used Greek word.

The Greek word *proskuneo* is found in 75% of the verses. *Proskuneo* is used in John 4:20-24, the key passage to understanding what Jesus taught about worship. It is also found in the book of Revelation to describe the act of worship in the throne room of God.

The Greek scholar Spiros Zodhiates vividly described the cultural meaning of *proskuneo*. In Middle Eastern societies, especially Persia which had exerted much influence over the region, the ancient mode of greeting one another was determined by rank:

---

1   See Appendix A for a complete list of these verses.
2   See Appendix B for a complete list of these verses.

Persons of equal rank kissed each other on the lips. When the difference of rank was slight, they kissed each other on the cheek. When one was much inferior, he fell upon his knees and touched his forehead to the ground or prostrated himself, throwing kisses at the same time towards the superior.

It is this latter mode of salutation that Greek writers expressed by *proskuneo*.[3]

Strong's Concordance defines it: 'to kiss like a dog licking his master's hand; to fawn or to crouch; to prostrate oneself in homage'. What are we to think of the meaning 'to kiss like a dog licking his master's hand'? It certainly creates an interesting word picture.

At my house there is always at least one dog in residence. When you have a well-trained dog, it is a satisfying experience to come home from work. You open the door, step in, and the dog runs up to you, careful to show obedience but more than ready to show affection to its master. How does it do that? Our dog will gladly lick the hand that is extended towards her.

I risk stretching this analogy a bit too far, but bear with me. It seems a beautiful picture of our worship under the New Covenant. Like the obedient dog, we approach our Master with the same respect, fear and submission of the Old Testament worshiper. At the same time, because of what Christ did for us we are free to express our love and adoration to the Father. I suppose we should be thankful that *proskuneo* referred to dogs rather than cats!

Face-down worship

The physical act of prostration, flat on one's face, was required whenever a worshiper was in the presence of God, Jesus or an

---

3   Spiros Zodhiates, *The Complete Word Study Dictionary*, New Testament, 1992, p.1233.

angel representing them.[4] When the Lord appeared to men of old, they bowed down flat on the ground in fear, knowing God was so holy that their lives were threatened. In the presence of Jesus, men and women fell down before him because he was sent from God, as witnessed by the miracles and the power of his words.

The last instance of Christians *proskuneo*-worshiping Jesus while he was on earth may be found in Matthew 28. Jesus appeared to the disciples on a mountaintop shortly before he ascended to heaven and they worshiped him.[5] When Jesus appeared from heaven to Paul and John, their reactions were instinctive and proper: in fear and reverence, they immediately fell down to the ground.[6] Only once more is *proskuneo* mentioned in a Christian gathering. In 1 Corinthians 14, an unbeliever is convicted of his sin and he performs the act of *proskuneo* to God.[7]

There are no other instances of *proskuneo* worship to God or Jesus until Revelation chapter 4 at the great throne-room scene. For Christians today, God is not physically present when we worship. Neither is Jesus. He is seated at the right hand of God in the heavenly throne room.

For these reasons, and because of the amazing change in worship from a physical place on earth to the inner spiritual person, I believe *proskuneo* is not *required* as our physical, external response to God while on earth. There is certainly nothing wrong with practicing face-down worship. But we cannot require others to perform it in public or private devotions, and those who do it are no more spiritual or accepted by God than those who don't.

I hope we can agree that, far beyond the physical form of it, *proskuneo* teaches us the right attitude for worship in spirit and truth. We should offer the total submission of our minds, our hearts and our flesh to God. This is the heart of worship.

---

4   There are many verses that teach this. Representative are Genesis 18:1-2; Genesis 19:1; Exodus 34:6-8; Daniel 10:1-15; Matthew 2:11; Matthew 8:2; Matthew 14:33; Revelation 7:11.
5   Matthew 28:17.
6   Acts 9:4; Revelation 1:17.
7   1 Corinthians 14:24-25.

What would King James think?

King James was more familiar with Zodhiates' description of worship than with our contemporary meanings. When a commoner entered the throne room of England in 1611, he would not dare to stroll down the center of the room toward the king, waving hello and smiling.

Such a person would be presumptuous, acting as if they were on equal terms with the king. He could lose his head for lack of respect. No, that person approached the throne slowly and reverently, bowing several times and scraping low to the ground, and never daring to look the king directly in the eyes until permission was granted.

Unlike that trembling subject of King James who feared sudden death for making a mistake as he worshiped, there is great news for the Christian worshiper. Christians need never fear the wrath and anger of God as we worship him in the ways that please him. Jesus is 'able to save to the uttermost those who come to God through Him, since He always lives to make intercession for them.'[8]

This should promote feelings of gratitude in every Christian, and give us the desire to learn what pleases God the Father. Through Jesus, God loves us and has promised to deliver us from the terrible wrath he will inflict upon his enemies. 'For God so loved the world that He gave His only begotten Son, that whoever believes in Him should not perish but have everlasting life.'[9] Amen!

Jesus is now seated in the throne room of God,[10] representing us to the Father as our advocate.[11] Think of it as having the perfect defense lawyer who will always please the judge, or the perfect ambassador who will always please the king — and always for our good. Yet when we try to approach God in ways that are

---

8   Hebrews 7:25.
9   John 3:16.
10   Hebrews 8:1; 12:2.
11   1 John 2:1.

not pleasing to him, we must also be willing to accept correction from the Lord.[12]

Acts of worship

If *proskuneo* is for the inner person and we are not required to fall down flat on our faces, what about outward or physical acts of worship? What does the New Testament teach us about visible acts of worship?

The New Testament uses another Greek word for worship that means 'to offer religious service to God'. This describes external acts of worship and is applied to Christians in several passages.[13]

The word *latreuo* (and the derivative *latreia*) comes from *latris*, a servant hired to work in a temple and perform the religious duties of worship. In English translations, *latreuo* and *latreia* are usually rendered 'served' or 'service'. However, in two key verses, Romans 12:1 and Hebrews 12:28, the NIV and the ESV (two modern translations popular within contemporary worship circles) diverged and rendered it 'worship'.

This word was originally used in Greek literature to describe the hired servants of pagan temples who performed the religious rites. We get the word 'idolatry' from the Greek '*eido-latreia*' — which literally means the religious service given to images representing false gods. In the Septuagint version of the Old Testament written in Greek, *latreuo* was used to describe the worship acts that were commanded by God in the Law and performed by the priests of Israel.

However, when the context refers to Christians, this religious service should be viewed first and foremost as a *spiritual* worship, not simply the performance of external rites. The

---

12 Hebrews 12:10.
13 Matthew 4:10; Acts 24:14; Acts 27:23; Romans 1:9; Philippians 3:3; 2 Timothy 1:3; Hebrews 9:14; Hebrews 12:28.

apostle Peter called us 'a holy priesthood, to offer up *spiritual* sacrifices acceptable to God through Jesus Christ'.[14] Paul described Christians as the ones 'who worship [*latreuo*] God in the Spirit, rejoice in Christ Jesus, and have no confidence in the flesh'.[15]

Later in the book, we will discover New Covenant sacrifices that are acceptable to God. We will learn how the right internal/spiritual worship produces external/physical acts of worship that are pleasing to God.

The God-fearer

There is one more important type of worshiper found in the New Testament. We meet this group in Antioch of Pisidia on the Sabbath at the synagogue. Paul was invited to speak by the Jewish leaders and he began his address, 'Men of Israel, and *you who fear God*, listen.'[16]

The 'God-fearers' were Gentile proselytes, pagans newly converted to the Jewish religion. The men had not yet been circumcised, but the men and women had all renounced idolatry to serve the true God and were permitted to worship in the synagogues.

The Greek word used for this worship is *sebomai*, meaning to revere; to adore; devout, religious worship. Originally meaning a bodily movement of falling backwards, this type of worship was expressed by an attitude of respect and by visibly being impressed by someone great and lofty.

Lydia of Thyatira was the best-known example of this type of worshiper.[17] Other examples of God-fearing Gentiles were

---

14   1 Peter 2:5.
15   Philippians 3:3.
16   Acts 13:16.
17   Acts 16:14.

Cornelius[18] and Titius Justus.[19] A related Greek word is *eusebes* (or *eusebo*). It is used to describe Cornelius as a devout man,[20] and by Paul to instruct Timothy and Titus that Christians are to live godly and pious lives.[21]

Paul brought the message of the gospel to these God-fearing Gentiles, proclaiming that Jesus Christ was the promised light to the Gentiles and that through Christ — not the Law of Moses — they could be saved. They enthusiastically embraced the gospel, believed on Christ, and were baptized.

So the first Gentile converts to Christianity were already devout worshipers of the true God. Through Christ, their worship was instantly changed from the rituals of the Jews to worship in spirit and truth.

A secret to pleasing God

It might seem that we are completely free from the 'fear of God' worship of the Jews and these first Gentile converts. Nothing could be further from the truth, and nothing is more dangerous for a Christian to believe than that! We can learn something vital from the first Gentile converts, the God-fearers.

The New Testament worshiper must still show respect for God's holy and righteous character. Learning a proper fear of God is a vital lesson for the twenty-first-century Christian, especially those who were raised under a different type of worship where only God's love and grace are emphasized. Here are some lessons to get you started.

- 'Let us cleanse ourselves from all filthiness of the flesh and spirit, perfecting holiness in the fear of God.'[22]

---

18 Acts 10:2; 10:22.
19 Acts 18:7.
20 Acts 10:2.
21 2 Timothy 3:12; Titus 2:12.
22 2 Corinthians 7:1.

- 'Conduct yourselves throughout the time of your stay here in fear.'[23]
- 'And do not fear those who kill the body but cannot kill the soul. But rather fear Him who is able to destroy both soul and body in hell.'[24]
- 'Fear God. Honor the king.'[25]
- 'But in every nation whoever fears Him and works righteousness is accepted by Him.'[26]
- 'Knowing, therefore, the terror of the Lord, we persuade men.'[27]
- 'Then a voice came from the throne, saying, "Praise our God, all you His servants and those who fear Him, both small and great!"'[28]

The book of Hebrews is a great place to learn more about worship. The book explains how the old sacrificial worship system was made obsolete by Jesus' sacrifice, once for all. As you study the tabernacle, which was a shadow of the heavenly sanctuary where God dwells,[29] you cannot escape the overwhelming sense of awe and reverence that was required for anyone who approached the tabernacle.

By the time you arrive at Hebrews chapter 10, the old way to approach God is gone for ever and replaced by the blood of Jesus Christ. We receive the great news that we have 'boldness to enter the Holiest by the blood of Jesus.'[30]

Some have taken this concept of 'boldness' as their excuse for allowing into Christian worship all types of profane practices borrowed from the pagan culture. Perhaps in anticipation that future generations would get careless with their worship and

23 1 Peter 1:17.
24 Matthew 10:28.
25 1 Peter 2:17.
26 Acts 10:35.
27 2 Corinthians 5:11.
28 Revelation 19:5.
29 Hebrews 8:5.
30 Hebrews 10:19.

forget to properly respect God, we were given Hebrews 12:28-29. There we are commanded to offer God acceptable worship, 'with reverence and awe, for our God is a consuming fire'.[31] Worship is translated from *latreuo*; some Bible versions say 'serve God'.

What is meant by 'acceptable' worship? The Greek word for acceptable is *euarestôs* which carries the idea of something that is fully pleasing to God. And what exactly pleases God here? Acts of religious service and devotion offered with a proper sense of reverence and awe.

Awe

Awe — I think we have lost the sense of what that really means. 'Awesome' was downgraded at the end of the twentieth century to mean 'really cool' in American slang. Through Hollywood movies and American pop music, the rest of the world thinks 'awesome' is a great compliment for coolness.

But the meaning here is so far from that. The AV translates it as godly fear! There is nothing 'cool' about a consuming fire. Awe properly belongs to God and God alone.[32] Consider how one Bible commentator described the fear of God from a Christian viewpoint:

> A holy veneration or fear is always an elementary principle of religion. It is the fear not so much of punishment by God, as the fear of earning God's disapproval. Not so much the dread of suffering, as it is the dread of doing wrong.[33]

In other words, when we sin, Christians should fear the disapproval of their Heavenly Father. We fear him not only out

---

31 Hebrews 12:28-29 (ESV).
32 Job 25:2; Isaiah 29:23; Jeremiah 2:19; Luke 5:26.
33 Albert Barnes' *Commentary* on 1 Peter 2:17.

of love and respect for his honor, but because there are real consequences when we disobey our Father. He disciplines every one of us.[34]

Reverence

We like to talk today about 'reverent' worship, but do we know what reverence means anymore? *Aidos*, the other Greek word used in Hebrews 12:28, gives us insight into the reverent attitude that is fully pleasing to God. *Aidos* is used only one other time in the New Testament. In 1 Timothy, it is translated 'shamefacedness'[35] and refers to the modesty and humility that adorns a godly woman.

What a picture for all of us to keep in mind as we worship God acceptably. In Philippians 4:8, we are instructed to keep our minds fixed on whatever things are noble. Translated from an old Greek work that is related to *sebomai*, noble means the things that inspire reverence and respect for God.

Finally, Hebrews 12:29 reminds us why our worship to God here on earth must always be conducted with reverence and godly fear. Our God is still a consuming fire. The reference comes from Deuteronomy 4:24 and it refers to the First and Second Commandments where God commanded his people never to have any other gods before him because 'I, the LORD your God, am a jealous God.'[36]

Summary

In this chapter, we learned that worship is not anything we dream it or wish it to be. Worship has very specific meanings

---

34   Job 5:17; Proverbs 3:11; Hebrews 12:7-8.
35   1 Timothy 2:9 (AV).
36   Exodus 20:5.

in the Bible. Biblical worship does not change to suit us; we are changed to suit biblical worship.

From a study of worship passages, we can draw several principles.

- The most common biblical act of worship was to bow down flat on one's face.
- The vast majority of worship passages in the Bible make no mention of music, even in context.
- Worship in spirit involves a heart attitude of total submission to our King.
- Worship in truth involves obedience to the commandments of God and Christ.
- Our worship is pleasing to God when it is offered with a grateful attitude of reverence and awe.
- Biblical meanings of worship do not include the pleasure or blessings of the worshiper. Everything is directed to what pleases and blesses God.

Knowing this, we should examine every practice we call 'worship' and align it with the Scriptures. We should keep those practices that closely conform, and discard those things that do not. What are the practices that best reflect a submissive heart and an obedient will? God has told us what they are.

Chapter 4

Did you remember to sacrifice today?

With a good understanding of biblical worship, now we are ready to answer the big question from chapter 2: how should I worship God?

I would imagine that you were not expecting to see anything about offering sacrifices. Aren't Christians free from the Law and no longer required to offer sacrifices as part of our worship to God? Didn't we settle that in the previous chapters, when we learned how Jesus offered one sacrifice for sins for ever and put an end to the daily sacrifices at the temple?[1]

Yes, Jesus put an end to God's requirement for sacrifices to cover our sins. Those animal sacrifices were never able to 'cleanse your conscience from dead works to serve the living God'.[2] Only the blood of Christ could do that and reconcile us to God the Father.

But did you know that God still expects us to offer sacrifices that please him? You may be surprised to learn that the New Testament teaches this clearly and openly. It is not a mystery at all. The mystery is how we have missed this in our endless discussions and debates about worship.

---

1   Hebrews 10:12.
2   Hebrews 9:14.

Why sacrifice?

To recap from chapter 2, from the beginning of recorded time worship has fundamentally been about pleasing God by offering sacrifices. After sin entered the world, God commanded his earliest followers to worship him through sacrifices of animals and food.

Consider the first recorded act of worship all the way back in Genesis 4. Abel killed the first-born from his flock of sheep, brought it before God, and the Lord accepted it. When the great floodwaters receded and Noah left the ark, the first thing he did was build 'an altar to the LORD, and took of every clean animal and of every clean bird, and offered burnt offerings on the altar.'[3]

Abraham built altars to the Lord in the land of Canaan[4] and the Hebrew word for altar[5] implies that he sacrificed animals there. When God established his covenant with Abraham, it was marked by the blood-spilt sacrifice of several animals.[6] In God's ultimate test of obedience and faith, Abraham was prepared to sacrifice his son Isaac as a burnt-offering on an altar. But God provided a ram for the sacrifice.[7]

God's people were not the only ones who sacrificed. Pagan religions that originated from Cain's descendants copied and then corrupted the true worship to God, turning instead to false gods of heaven or earth. Pagan worshipers sacrificed animals and food, and even humans, to their false gods in a vain hope of pleasing them and receiving blessings.

Whatever blessings fell upon the pagans were not a result of their sacrifices or their gods. Their gods were dumb idols of stone[8] and their sacrifices and pleadings for help fell on deaf

---

3   Genesis 8:20.
4   Genesis 12:7-8; 13:18.
5   The Hebrew word *mizbach* comes from *zabach* — to slay.
6   Genesis 15:9-10.
7   Genesis 22:1-14.
8   1 Corinthians 12:2.

ears.[9] The true God reminded us that he 'in bygone generations allowed all nations to walk in their own ways. Nevertheless He did not leave Himself without witness, in that He did good, gave us rain from heaven and fruitful seasons, filling our hearts with food and gladness'.[10]

Later when the Law was given, God's people were required to sacrifice the best of their animals as a sin offering and to offer the first fruits of their crops as peace offerings. As a nation, Israel was required to sacrifice bulls and goats every single day of the year for the sins of the people. We learn from these examples that the worship of God has included real sacrifice from the beginning.

Once for all

Thanks be to Jesus Christ, our sins were forgiven at the cross when he shed his precious blood and satisfied God's righteous demand for justice once and for all. That means believers in Jesus Christ as Lord and Savior are sanctified, and their sins are forgiven by God on account of Jesus. Therefore, we are no longer required to offer animal sacrifices to atone for our sins. Furthermore, Jesus made peace with God for us, so we are no longer required to sacrifice food as peace-offerings to an angry God.[11] Hallelujah!

But did that mean we were freed of *all* sacrifices to God? Can we simply sit around all day and meditate silently in our hearts, souls and minds, worshiping in spirit and in truth? The answer is both yes *and* no.

Yes, our inner worship of God is spiritual,[12] and the first and most important thing is to serve him with our spirit. But no,

---

9   1 Kings 18:25-29.
10   Acts 14:16-17.
11   Ephesians 2:11-22.
12   John 4:20-24.

we can't stop there and claim 'It's only what is in my heart that matters'. Our external behavior is a result of what we love in our hearts. It is what a man believes in his heart that defiles or honors him; the results are often displayed for others to see.[13]

Perhaps to demonstrate his glory to a skeptical world, God asked Christians to continue offering some very specific sacrifices. This is where we can discover the 'how to' of Christian worship and find out what worship practices are acceptable, or well pleasing, to God.

Summary

The following chapters will reveal three sacrifices that God expects from New Testament worshipers:

1. The sacrifice of my body;
2. The sacrifice of praise;
3. The sacrifice of koinonia.

This is a worthwhile journey to take. At the end of it, we can spend our time focused on things that please God, rather than wasting time on all the other things we have added to please ourselves or to follow the teachings of men.

---

13   Matthew 15:11; Mark 7:20.

Chapter 5

The sacrifice of my body

I beseech you therefore, brethren, by the mercies of God, that you present your bodies a living sacrifice, holy, acceptable to God, which is your reasonable service.[1]

Worship has always involved a sacrifice of something or someone. Worship and sacrifice are still inseparable. Gory and medieval as it may seem to our twenty-first-century sensibilities, the fact is that a death was required to please God.

Thanks be to Jesus — we don't have to slaughter an animal to worship God today. But a physical sacrifice is still required by God. That is what Romans 12:1 is all about. We should be grateful that we are a 'living' sacrifice, not a dead one.

What does this mean, practically speaking? How can your body become a sacrifice while it is still alive? This can be confusing! Let's work through it together.

---

1   Romans 12:1.

Not your body anymore

When you became a Christian, your body became the property of God and he sent the Holy Spirit to live in his new property. 'Do you not know that your body is the temple of the Holy Spirit who is in you, whom you have from God, and you are not your own? For you were bought at a price; therefore glorify God in your body and in your spirit, which are God's.'[2]

God has first rights to your body and expects you to honor his ownership. That means you are not permitted to use it anymore for 'doing what the Gentiles want to do, living in sensuality, passions, drunkenness, orgies, drinking parties, and lawless idolatry.'[3] Instead, 'just as you used to offer the parts of your body in slavery to impurity and to ever-increasing wickedness, so now offer them in slavery to righteousness leading to holiness.'[4]

We worship God acceptably with our bodies when we obey his commandments and strive to live for righteousness. This is a life lived separate from many worldly pleasures. However, the reward is worth it! The word 'acceptable' in Romans 12:1 is translated from the Greek word *euarestos*. It means that God is 'well pleased' with our sacrifice. We can delight and take joy in pleasing our Heavenly Father.

Cross walk

Here is how 'death while living' works. Jesus taught that 'whoever commits sin is a slave of sin', but 'the truth shall make you free.'[5] When we were converted to Christ, spiritually speaking we died to sin and are slaves no more. The old man was 'crucified with

---

2   1 Corinthians 6:19-20.
3   1 Peter 4:3 (ESV).
4   Romans 6:19 (NIV).
5   John 8:32-36.

Him, that the body of sin might be done away with, that we should no longer be slaves of sin.'[6]

Before Jesus was crucified, he was forced to take up his own cross and walk to his death. 'Do you not know that as many of us as were baptized into Christ Jesus were baptized into His death?'[7] But Jesus defeated death so all believers can have eternal life through him. Today we have been given this new and righteous life *spiritually*. But while we are on the earth in our bodies of flesh, there is a constant struggle between the old nature and the new.[8]

I think that explains why Jesus said that each disciple would have to 'take up his cross daily.'[9] Every day when I symbolically take up my cross and walk to my death, I die to self. My body is reckoned to be dead to 'fornication, uncleanness, passion, evil desire, and covetousness, which is idolatry.'[10] I am to offer it instead to God as a living sacrifice, holy and pleasing.

Verse 2 is there for a purpose

In the second verse of Romans 12, we are given a practical blueprint of how to keep our bodies under control and maintain a sacrifice acceptable for worship. It is a classic case of mind over matter. 'For as he thinks in his heart, so is he.'[11] It helps to read Romans 12:2 in reverse order:

1. To discern what God's will is for your sacrifice,
2. and to know what is fully agreeable (pleasing) to him,
3. then you must be transformed by the renewing of your mind,

---

6   Romans 6:6.
7   Romans 6:2,3.
8   Romans 7:24.
9   Luke 9:23.
10   Colossians 3:5.
11   Proverbs 23:7.

4. so that the things you do in the body will no longer be conformed to and fashioned by the spirit of this age.

The Greek word translated 'conformed to' is *suschematizo* and the English word 'schematic' comes from it. The seventeenth-century nonconformist theologian Matthew Poole described this conformance in terms very relevant for today:

> Do not fashion or accommodate yourselves to the corrupt principles, customs, or courses of worldly and wicked men; and what they are, you will find in Romans 13:13, Ephesians 4:18,19 and 1 Peter 4:3.[12]

Spiros Zodhiates, a contemporary Greek scholar who was very familiar with the present age we live in, taught that we should 'stop being molded by the external and fleeting fashions of this age and undergo a deep inner change'.[13]

Albert Barnes explained conformity to the world in clear terms:

> Christians should not conform to the maxims, habits, and feelings of a wicked, luxurious, and idolatrous age, but should be conformed solely to the precepts and laws of the gospel. The same principle may be extended to every age, and the direction may be that Christians should not conform to the prevailing habits, style, and manners of the world — the people who know not God.[14]

What should a Christian conform to instead? In Romans 8:29, we are taught that God in his sovereign grace has already decided to conform us to the image of his Son in order that we may be saved and justified. Someday God himself will transform

---

12 Matthew Poole's *Commentary*.
13 Zodhiates, *The Complete Word Study Dictionary*, New Testament, p.1350.
14 Albert Barnes' *NT Commentary*.

our lowly bodies so they may be conformed to Christ's glorious body and we will live for ever in heaven.[15] Amen!

Keeping our bodies from being conformed to this world does not save us or justify us before God. But that does not excuse us from doing our duty to God. While we are in this world, Romans 12:1-2 clearly teaches that a holy body is an act of obedience to the will of God and to his commandments. This is our reasonable act of worship that pleases God and keeps us from much trouble in this world.

At war

The members of the body are constantly waging war against the mind.[16] Therefore it is necessary for our minds to undergo a contin-uous renovation process; that is what renewing[17] literally means in verse 2. The renovation and renewal project is done by God's Word, which is 'a discerner of the thoughts and intents of the heart'.[18] We are washed clean with the Word[19] and sanctified by it.[20]

A mind not constantly renewed can easily become a mind set on earthly things, and fall into believing that the fashions of this age are not so bad after all. That mind can slip further into believing that 'intellectually' we might conform to some of its fashions and styles without any of the physical repercussions which might defile our living sacrifice.

But whenever one plays with idols, there is always a back-sliding away from God and into sins of the flesh. Many believers now walk as if they are enemies to the cross, because their minds are set on earthly things.[21]

---

15 Philippians 3:21.
16 Romans 7:23.
17 Greek — *anakainôsei*.
18 Hebrews 4:12.
19 Ephesians 5:26.
20 John 17:17.
21 Philippians 3:17-19.

What does this dangerous conformity look like? I realize it is always perilous to 'name the sin' and make generalizations that apply to all Christians. Therefore I offer the following scenarios only as examples with which I am familiar.

Zeitgeist or Christ?

For example, a Christian may decide to drink alcohol socially because the Scriptures do not absolutely forbid alcohol consumption. But social drinking is the fashion of this age and every age. He believes he can control himself. But soon he finds his body in terrible trouble, because wine is a mocker, strong drink a brawler, and whoever is intoxicated by it is not wise.[22] He ends up spending his spare time in wicked places he never thought he would enter. Alcohol poisons his flesh to the point of sickness. He never imagined he would smoke pot but alcohol broke down his inhibitions. His body is no longer a holy sacrifice and acceptable worship.

Or a Christian thinks she can enjoy rock music without limits, because a Christian leader told her that music is neutral and simply listening for enjoyment will never lead to sin in her body. But sensual and rebellious music styles are the soundtrack of this wicked age. In time she dresses in very immodest clothes similar to a prostitute, dances immorally like a stripper, and gets a 'tramp stamp' tattoo. Her body is no longer a holy sacrifice and acceptable worship.

Or a Christian believes that following sports is an innocent pursuit. But to be a sports fanatic ('fan' for short) is another fashion of this age. The fan's mind becomes overwhelmed by statistics and records, and he is consumed by winning and losing and watching sports on TV. In time, the Christian 'fan' ignores his family and spends a fortune on sporting activities

---

22 Proverbs 20:1.

and paraphernalia. Sports become his god. His body is no longer a holy sacrifice and acceptable worship, because he is too busy serving the god of sports.

Or a young Christian man relaxes at the beach among almost-nude young women. He was encouraged by a famous preacher who said that God made women beautiful and exposing their bodies is not a sin unless a man lusts in his heart. But public indecency and the baring of flesh are very much a fashion of this age. In time this young man is overcome by lust and is caught up in sexual immorality. His body is no longer a holy sacrifice and acceptable worship.

These examples demonstrate how a mind set on earthly things can lead to a body that is unholy and unacceptable as a sacrifice to God. Our worship can be rendered useless if we let our guard down, dabble with the fashions and styles of this present age, and fall into dishonorable and impure behavior with our bodies.

Summary

When do we sacrifice our bodies to the Lord? Daily as we take up our cross, die to self and follow Jesus. We can do this through a simple prayer. Where does this act of worship happen? The answer is found in this verse: 'Do you not know that your body is the temple of the Holy Spirit who is in you, whom you have from God?'[23] It happens wherever you take the temple.

How are we doing with this first sacrifice? If we aren't paying attention to this one, everything else we offer God could be worthless.

---

23 1 Corinthians 6:19.

Chapter 6

The sacrifice of praise

Therefore by Him let us continually offer the sacrifice of praise to God, that is, the fruit of our lips, giving thanks to His name ... for with such sacrifices God is well pleased.[1]

All the musicians must be relieved that we have finally come to the part of the journey about music. Here is the classic verse that supports music as an acceptable act of worship for the Christian. It is a sacrifice that pleases God.

The sacrifice of praise is a continuous offering and involves the confession of God's name as a way to show our gratitude to him. In the Old Testament, a similar offering was the Towdah or thank-offering, made to God with public confession of his power, goodness and mercy. Towdah comes from the Hebrew *yadah*, which means to confess God. It is usually translated as a sacrifice of thanksgiving or praise. The Psalms are our primary source for direction on the Old Testament version of this offering:

---

1   Hebrews 13:15,16b.

- 'That I may proclaim with the voice of thanksgiving [towdah], and tell of all Your wondrous works.'[2]
- 'Offer to God thanksgiving [towdah], and pay your vows to the Most High.'[3]
- 'Whoever offers praise [towdah] glorifies Me.'[4]
- 'I will praise the name of God with a song, and will magnify Him with thanksgiving [towdah].'[5]
- 'Let us come before His presence with thanksgiving [towdah]; let us shout joyfully to Him with psalms.'[6]
- 'Enter into His gates with thanksgiving [towdah], and into His courts with praise. Be thankful to Him, and bless His name.'[7]
- 'Let them sacrifice the sacrifices of thanksgiving [towdah), and declare His works with rejoicing.'[8]
- 'I will offer to You the sacrifice of thanksgiving (towdah], and will call upon the name of the LORD.'[9]
- 'Sing to the LORD with thanksgiving [towdah]; sing praises on the harp to our God.'[10]

All about music?

We could finish here and declare it's all about the music. Not so fast. The 'sacrifice of praise' in Hebrews 13:15 is qualified by a most curious phrase, 'the fruit of our lips'. Now what does that mean?

The 'fruit of lips' refers back to Hosea 14:2. This reference is *not* talking about happy, clappy praise music by the temple choir. The subject matter is sobering.

---

2   Psalm 26:7.
3   Psalm 50:14.
4   Psalm 50:23.
5   Psalm 69:30.
6   Psalm 95:2.
7   Psalm 100:4.
8   Psalm 107:22.
9   Psalm 116:17.
10 Psalm 147:7.

Return, O Israel, to the Lord your God,
For you have stumbled because of your iniquity.
Take words with you and return to the Lord.
Say to Him, 'Take away all iniquity,
And receive us graciously,
that we may present the fruit of our lips.'[11]

In this passage, God said he would not accept their animal or grain sacrifices. Instead he wanted to hear prayers of repentance from sin — the words from their lips as the sacrifice. This reference adds a vital new dimension to our understanding of the sacrifice of praise. Let's learn more about it.

Sacrifice of prayer

The sacrifice of praise is not simply about offering joyous music with triumphant lyrics. This sacrifice is first about our prayers of confession. The words that come from our lips are the most important part of the offering.

Take note of how Hebrews 13:15 begins: by or through Jesus, we offer up this sacrifice. Does that not sound like an instruction for prayer, more than instruction for music? We pray to God in Jesus' name and our offering must go through him, for no man comes to the Father but by him. Jesus is the mediator between God and man.[12]

When we compare this with the entire book of Hebrews, the sacrifice of praise as prayer — not music — starts to make more sense. When we draw near to God through Christ and boldly approach the throne of grace, it is not for the purpose of offering music. It is to offer prayers for mercy and grace.[13]

---

11   Hosea 14:2 (NASB).
12   1 Timothy 2:5.
13   Hebrews 4:16.

In Hebrews 4:16, 'boldly' does not mean to come to the throne with loud music and happy dancing, or any music for that matter. It means to come to God with freedom of speech, holding no confessions back from him.[14] Because Christ is our mediator to God, we can confess our sins with freedom from fear of God's judgement. We can frankly and openly plead with God for help. In return, we can expect to receive mercy and find grace in our time of need. What a great encouragement!

Prayer becomes praise

We tend to think of the Psalms as a songbook. Many Christians are consumed with curiosity about the original music of the Psalms, trying to decipher if there are musical terms hidden there and what tunes David and Asaph used. Rick Warren used Psalm 40:3 to justify the change to modern worship music in his Purpose-Driven Church. Arguments even rage over whether or not the modern drum set was foretold in Psalm 150!

Once again, our extravagant affection for music has clouded our vision, and we are missing the point. I would like you to look at the Psalms with a fresh set of eyes. Discover them anew as the inspired prayer book of words for the worshiper of God.

Within the Psalms, every verbal expression of praise to God has been modeled for us. We can pray with the very words God gave us: 'Take words with you, and return to the LORD.'[15] We can never exhaust this treasury of words to speak and sing back to God.

What about praising Jesus? The Psalms do look forward to the Messiah in several passages but the name of Jesus is not explicitly found there. This, along with the doggerel verse in the *Whole Booke of Psalmes*, caused young Isaac Watts to complain

---

14 Greek *parrhesia*.
15 Hosea 14:2.

about the poor singing at Above Bar Independent Church in Southampton, England.

His father wisely counseled him: 'Try then, whether you can do something better.' Watts took up the challenge and began to rewrite the Psalter with Christian themes. Thus was born the Christian hymn of praise as we know it today.[16] His revolution was not about changing the music; Watts was all about using the right words!

Many great hymns started as a sacred prayer poem written by a godly person, in the holy tradition of the psalmist. Set into meter, the poem can then be matched to an appropriate tune and now the prayer may be sung, and prayer becomes a hymn of praise.

We can also find prayers in the New Testament that praise Jesus in a poetic form similar to the Psalms. The 'Worthy is the Lamb' song in Revelation[17] and the great praise passage to Christ found in Philippians chapter 2[18] are wonderful examples of Christian hymns embedded in there.

The point is that our sacrifice of praise begins and ends with the words God gave us. If there is one thing you learn from this book, let it be that biblical praise is all about the words, not the music. Praise must be centered first around fitting and honorable words.

But how many modern worship songs are created first as a 'cool' musical groove, and then the words are added later? Read the online interviews of today's popular worship music artists, and learn how often they write a song by first creating the music and then the words come to them. This is the craft of the pop music singer-songwriter who cares most about musical sounds and rhythms.

Praise does not have to include music. Any spoken words that exalt God and Jesus qualify as the sacrifice of praise — the

---

16   Faith Cook, *Our hymn-writers and their hymns*, pp.44-45.
17   Revelation 5:12.
18   Philippians 2:5-11.

fruit of our lips. Reading the Bible aloud and praying out loud in church or in private are acceptable sacrifices of praise. Make a joyful noise[19] unto the Lord and you have praised him.

Pray more

What, then, does this mean for our worship? First, before we sing in private or public worship, let us not neglect our prayers of confession to God. There is evidence that the early church understood this when they gathered for worship.

> But every Lord's day, *give thanksgiving after having confessed your transgressions, that your sacrifice may be pure.* But let no one that is at variance with his fellow come together with you, until they be reconciled, that your sacrifice may not be profaned.[20]

Second, we must bring our offering through Christ. This is essential to understand. God does not accept a sacrifice of praise from a person who is not a believer in Christ. Be careful the musicians in your worship service are all believers, or they play and sing in vain.

Here then we have the right model for the sacrifice of praise. Continually confess your sins in spoken prayer and reconcile differences with your brethren. Sing your happy praise songs only after you have done this, and your sacrifice of praise will be acceptable to God.

Rare is the church today which follows this God-ordained process. Most start the worship service with an upbeat, happy-clappy song and move straight into a lengthy song package. If

---

19 Psalm 66:1; 81:1; 95:1; 95:2; 98:4; 98:6; 100:1 (AV). Joyful noise had nothing to do with singing loud rock music or any other rowdy style. It meant to shout loudly to the Lord in unison or loudly blow a trumpet note at a special time of the Jewish temple service.
20 *Teachings of the Twelve Apostles*, chapter 14.

there is any time set aside for confession and reconciliation, it usually comes later.

Consider how many songs we may have offered in vain. How often was the musical offering rejected by God because we were so presumptuous to think our passionate music performance matters more to him than our confessions? Some worship leaders or pastors may retort: 'You should come to the service prayed up and prepared to celebrate Jesus.' But that is not a good excuse for ignoring the biblical process for offering praise, and it overlooks the fact that most worshipers come in desperate need of confession before praise.

Instrumental praise

If words are essential for a sacrifice of praise, then what about instrumental praise offerings? Many churches, contemporary or traditional, are filled with instrumental music performances where no one is singing the words of praise. Does music without words fulfill the sacrifice of praise?

At my home church, we have several gifted violinists and pianists who take turns performing the offertory. For those unfamiliar with this term, an offertory typically consists of instrumental music played while the offering is collected. At many traditional churches, the organist plays the offertory.

When a well-known hymn tune is played, the words may come immediately to mind for many; just as the words pop into our minds when we hear the opening chords of a 'golden oldie'. But to be honest, when we hear instrumental music we are more likely to praise the sound of the music and the skill of the musician.

Proof of that is the common and fast-spreading practice at many churches today where instrumentalists are applauded at the end of the performance. Applause is a reliable indicator of whom the human heart is praising.

Does instrumental music fulfill the sacrifice of praise? Dr Craig Ralston, Chair of the Division of Fine Arts at Clearwater Christian College, has all the words projected on the screen for each instrumental song at his sacred concerts. Craig also projects the words of his vocal numbers to move the focus from himself onto the all-important words. This is a practice that should be imitated at every church. As a practical side effect, projecting words also prevents the use of purely instrumental music or any song that lacks good doctrine.

Sometimes we find ourselves to be more inspired and moved by the sounds of music than by the words themselves. Knowing now the vast superiority of the words of praise over the music when it comes to pleasing God, I find myself understanding more and more the odd and ancient confession of Augustine:

> I am moved, not by the singing but by *what* is sung — when they are sung with a clear and skillfully modulated voice. Yet when it happens that I am more moved by the singing than by what is sung, I confess myself to have sinned wickedly, and then I would rather not have heard the singing.[21]

I should make it very clear that I am not calling for an end to instrumental music in our churches. I think every musician who plays an instrument should do it to the glory of God. I only wish to point out that the sacrifice of praise requires words, not music alone.

Summary

The second sacrifice required of the Christian is a sacrifice of words, from our lips to God, first as a prayer of confession. Music's place is to help us praise God and Christ with these

---

21   Augustine's *Confessions*, chapter XXXIII.

words. Even that notable lover of music Martin Luther showed he knew the proper place of music when he was said to have remarked that 'Music is the handmaiden of theology.'

When should the sacrifice of praise be made? Continually — pray without ceasing.[22] Jesus taught the disciples that they ought to pray at all times and not to lose heart.[23] Let us keep on offering up this sacrifice, until the Lord comes back.

Where is the place to sacrifice? As with our bodies, this one is completely portable too. We can pray or sing our praises anywhere that we are. We need not wait until Sunday or other worship times to bring this offering to God.

However it is all the more sweet and encouraging to offer up this sacrifice together with other Christians in our public worship. God called the church a body made up of individual parts,[24] and we are encouraged in the faith when we bring the sacrifice of praise together.[25]

---

22 1 Thessalonians 5:17.
23 Luke 18:1.
24 Romans 12:4; 1 Corinthians 12:18.
25 Colossians 3:16; Ephesians 5:19.

Chapter 7

The sacrifice of koinonia

But do not forget to do good and to share, for with such sacrifices God is well pleased.[1]

This is the 'forgotten' act of worship. It is easy to focus on the first two sacrifices (body and praise) and completely overlook the third leg of the stool. We can fall into thinking that since our good works did not save us, then our good works are not important for worship after we're converted. But you know what happens to a two-legged stool. It simply can't stand up.

'To share' is translated from the Greek word '*koinonia*'. That is why I call this the sacrifice of *koinonia*. When the first church was organized on the day of Pentecost, the Christians devoted themselves to *koinonia* (fellowship).[2] What did first-century *koinonia* look like?

Life was extremely difficult for Christians in the first century. When a Jew became a Christian, his Jewish family would disown him and cut him off from their support. He could lose

---

1   Hebrews 13:16.
2   Acts 2:42.

his job, have his home confiscated, or be dragged off to prison by the likes of the fire-breathing persecutor Saul (before he was converted on the road to Damascus).[3] Famine, hunger and prison were constant stalkers of the early Christians.

Redefining fellowship

In the context of this suffering and poverty, Christian fellowship is defined in Acts chapter 2: 'and sold their possessions and goods, and divided them among all, as anyone had need'.[4] This is not the superficial 'fellowship' we practice today in our churches: the fellowship 'coffee' time before or after a service; the fellowship 'handshake' time during the service; or the fellowship hall where we eat our pot-luck meals.

Through the sacrifice of *koinonia*, God provided material support for the church of Jesus Christ and brought glory to his name. The Christian system of caring for one another was so successful, 'nor was there anyone among them who lacked; for all who were possessors of lands or houses sold them, and brought the proceeds of the things that were sold, and laid them at the apostles' feet; and they distributed to each as anyone had need'.[5]

Koinonia also brought unity to the church by placing the rich and the poor on the same level: 'Now the multitude of those who believed were of one heart and one soul; neither did anyone say that any of the things he possessed was his own, but they had all things in common'.[6] This was not communism as Karl Marx defined it; this was a voluntary sacrifice of love, sharing one's abundance with those who had none.

Koinonia is first to be offered to the brethren and then to

---

3   Acts 22:4.
4   Acts 2:45.
5   Acts 4:34-35.
6   Acts 4:32.

strangers. *Philadelphia* is the Greek word meaning 'love of the brethren'. Many times we are commanded to take care of the family of God. *Philoxenos* is the Greek word for 'hospitality' and literally means to show love for strangers who are away from home, by offering them shelter and food and taking care of the sick ones.[7] The good Samaritan is Jesus' example to us.[8]

The sacrifice of *koinonia* also replaced the old sacrificial system of bringing physical and material goods for worship. Instead of burning the bull and the ram on the altar, Christians can use the meat to feed the hungry, the hide for shoes, and the wool to clothe the naked. And as the priests of Israel were once fed by the meat and grain offerings, so today are the pastors and workers fed by the tithes and offerings we bring.

Pass the offering plate

The first-century churches in Macedonia[9] deserve the title of 'The Best Sacrifice of *Koinonia* Ever'. Sound boastful? The apostle Paul boasted about them long ago.

First, let's become familiar with the Macedonian environment of the first century A.D. Being a Christian in a Roman province was hard. Roman law was tolerant of all religions, but it was very intolerant of any religion such as Christianity that claimed to be exclusive. At times that intolerance broke out into full-scale, terrible persecutions of the church.

Pagan sacrifices were part of Roman society and woven deeply into the fabric of daily life. If you went to the marketplace to shop for food, at the entry gate to the market you were expected to burn incense in honor of a false god. As you entered your place of work, there was an altar where each worker was expected to bring a sacrifice so the gods would favor the

---

7   Hebrews 13:2; 1 Timothy 3:2; Titus 1:8.
8   Luke 10:29-37.
9   The territory which lay to the north of Greece.

business. If you served in the military, before battle you were expected to sacrifice to a pagan god.

But Christians were commanded to 'flee from idolatry'.[10] Christians were forbidden to worship any other god and therefore unable to make sacrifices to Zeus, local gods or to the god on earth — Caesar. That was enough to keep Christians out of the marketplace and out of work.

So the Macedonian Christians were suffering under Roman control. They lived in deep poverty under a great deal of persecution and pressure from the Roman government. Famine constantly stalked them. If anyone needed the good works of *koinonia* from other churches, the Macedonian church did.

What did they do? Beg Paul for help? Send out a fund-raising letter? Conduct a first-century share-a-thon? No. In an incredible display of love and sacrifice, the Macedonians instead begged Paul to allow them to give more to other poor saints! They were pleased 'to make a certain contribution for the poor among the saints who are in Jerusalem.'[11]

Paul boasted about Macedonia in the second letter to the church at Corinth. He used their example to encourage the Corinthians to dig deeper and fulfill their pledge to help the destitute saints in Jerusalem.

- 'Moreover, brethren, we make known to you the grace of God bestowed on the churches of Macedonia:
- 'that in a great trial of affliction the abundance of their joy and their deep poverty abounded in the riches of their liberality.
- 'For I bear witness that according to their ability, yes, and beyond their ability, they were freely willing,
- 'imploring us with much urgency that we would receive the gift and the fellowship [*koinonia*] of the ministering to the saints.'[12]

---

10   Acts 15:29; 1 Corinthians 10:14.
11   Romans 15:26.
12   2 Corinthians 8:1-4.

These Christians are the role models for our sacrifice of *koinonia* today. Praise God for the Macedonians. See that you abound in this gracious work also.[13]

A gift that keeps on giving

Paul's 'faith-promise' challenge to the Corinthians also included a list of benefits for a *koinonia*-minded church. Now I realize we shouldn't give to God's work merely to receive a blessing in return; but there is no doubt that Paul was using the promise of blessings to encourage more giving. He went on to write (paraphrased):

1. You will be made rich in every way, so that you can be generous on every occasion.
2. Your generosity will result in thanksgiving to God.
3. Because of the service by which you have proved yourselves, men will praise God.
4. In their prayers for you, their hearts will go out to you.[14]

Paul's exhortation may have reminded them of God's promise in the Psalms. A man who gives generously to the poor will possess a righteousness that endures for ever, and his name will be exalted in honor long after he is gone.[15]

Failure is not an option

Where Paul persuaded gently and added some sweeteners, the apostle John cut right to the point. He warned Christians of the absolute necessity to practice this act of worship: 'But whoever

---

13   2 Corinthians 8:7.
14   2 Corinthians 9:11-14.
15   Psalm 112:9.

has this world's goods, and sees his brother in need, and shuts up his heart from him, how does the love of God abide in him?'[16]

In other words, a person can perform the sacrifice of praise continually and keep his body pure for worship, and he may appear to everyone else as if he is a true worshiper. But if he consciously neglects to share his goods with other Christians who are needy and persecuted, this person is not a true worshiper of God and, worse, may not even be a Christian!

It is time to look in the mirror again. How are we doing with this sacrifice? Does our worship include generous giving to poor and persecuted Christians? Do we willingly share when a local church member has a need? There are many practical ways to get involved.

Many churches operate food banks. Our church has a deacons' fund. We take special collections for members who lost jobs in the current economic recession and cannot buy food or afford healthcare for their families. Some may lose a home to foreclosure through no fault of their own.

Support your missionaries! They bring worthy needs to our attention from far-away lands. Look for ministries that bring aid to truly destitute and persecuted Christians wherever they are found. There are so many opportunities to worship God acceptably in this vital area.

When and where should you offer the sacrifice of *koinonia*? The local church provides a biblical system by collecting tithes and offerings once a week. Make sure to take care of your local church needs first. With the Internet you can also share your gifts abroad twenty-four hours a day and seven days a week.

How much is enough? The Macedonians set the bar high, didn't they? Jesus also offered great advice in his teaching on the widow's mite: it's not how much you give, it's how much you have left over.[17]

---

16   1 John 3:17.
17   Mark 12:41-44.

Stop talking about it

When we offer our sacrifice, let us do it as Jesus commanded when he taught his disciples how to give alms. Alms-giving was an act of compassion towards the poor. God expected his people to take care of the poor among them and anyone who cheated the poor came under harsh judgement.[18] But the Jewish religious leaders added 'doctrines of men' to God's expectations and taught the people that alms-giving contributed to one's justification (today we call this 'works-based' salvation).

Christians know that salvation is by the grace of God, and justification cannot be earned by our works.[19] But observant Jews in Jesus' time would have believed that the more they gave, the more righteous they would become. This led some of them to make a big show[20] of their giving so everyone would see their righteousness. Some would even hire a musician to go before them and sound a trumpet blast to announce they were about to give an offering!

Jesus denounced this blatant exhibitionism, called them hypocrites (mere actors),[21] and taught us instead to give our offerings in secret. He told us: 'Do not let your left hand know what your right hand is doing.'[22] The act of charitable giving should be done as secretly as possible and we should forget about it after we have given, lest we fall into pride.

Interestingly some Christian celebrities today boast about their charitable acts in public. One famous preacher issued a press release to announce he was doing a 'reverse-tithe' by giving 90% of his book sales and speaking fees to charity, keeping only 10% to live on, and paying his church back for all the salary

---

18 Deuteronomy 15:7-11; Proverbs 14:31; Amos 8:4.
19 Ephesians 2:8-9.
20 Our English word theatrical comes from the Greek word used in Matthew 6:1.
21 Matthew 6:2. Hypocrite is what the Greeks called a stage player who acted under a mask, impersonating a character. There were two masks (or faces) in Greek drama. The word came to mean anyone who was a counterfeit or was 'two-faced'.
22 Matthew 6:3.

they gave him through the years. What a righteous man, many thought.

The editor of BeliefNet was happy to go before him and blow the trumpet. 'He reverse-tithes, giving away 90% and keeping 10%. Please contemplate all the religious figures who have gotten rich off their flock and pocketed the money. Who among you reverse-tithe or would, if you were rich? Every time I think about what he has done it makes me question whether I'm giving enough. That is a Christ-like example.'[23]

No, that is not Christ-like. This preacher sold over twenty-five million books and 10% of that is still a lot of money. In comparison, Jesus made do with only a few shekels. I personally thought it was a decent gesture from a man who was made rich by God's people, but he should have kept it secret.

Instead, he promoted his sacrifice of *koinonia* to the world (11,600 hits on Google at last count) and he receives the praise and glory for his offering, not God. The first rule about acceptable worship is that God will not share his praise or glory with another.[24]

Contemporary Christian musicians are eager to show us how much they care about giving. Every band has its favorite charity now, promoted on their website and at concerts. On one hand (the left?), it is good that they care and want to use their celebrity to raise money for charities. But can we blame the skeptics for seeing this as a modern-day example of hypocrites eager to be seen giving in public? Or as an attempt by some to balance their guilt for riches made from Christian worship with 'good works done before men'?

God will judge all of this in the end. Whatever you choose to give and however you choose to do it, do not forget the sacrifice of *koinonia* and give it in secret with joy! For with this sacrifice, God is well pleased.

---

23 Steven Waldman, Editor-In-Chief and Co-Founder of BeliefNet, posted at Huffingtonpost.com December 17, 2008.
24 Isaiah 42:8.

Summary

We have discovered the sacrifices of the true worshiper of God, and learned how each act of worship pleases God.

1. The sacrifice of my body
2. The sacrifice of praise
3. The sacrifice of *koinonia*

Sacrifices are an integral component of our worship. We cannot worship God acceptably without sacrificing. Sacrifices require ... sacrifice! The worship of God is work. I like how my Lutheran readers described it: worship is the work of the people.

Resist the popular voices which tell us that worship is all about enjoying God through whatever style you are most passionate about. That is twenty-first-century, me-monster narcissism.

It is time to look in the mirror once more. Are we devoting our time to the sacrifices that please God, or are we wasting time on other things called 'worship' that are not even found as acceptable offerings?

Chapter 8

Worshipers who meet to worship

Were it not for public worship, private worship would soon be at an end. To this, the church of Christ owes its being and its continuance. Where there is no public worship, there is no religion. It is by this that God is acknowledged that he is the universal Being, and by his bounty and providence all live. Consequently, it is the duty of every intelligent creature to publicly acknowledge him, and offer him that worship which he himself has prescribed in his word.[1]

Until now, our discussion of worship has focused on our personal devotion to God. It is essential for us to get it right before we come together in public worship services. We must literally be the true worshipers in spirit and truth who come together for worship, or we risk wasting our time together.

Early Church Father Hippolytus described how Christians should prepare for public worship:

Let each one be diligent in coming to the church, the place where the Holy Spirit flourishes. If there is a day when there

---

1   Adam Clarke's *Commentary* on Hebrews 10:39.

is no instruction, let each one, when he is at home, take up a holy book and read in it...[2]

Wherever Christians assemble together for public worship, we follow an order of service. Even so-called 'spontaneous' churches, who abhor any rules of meeting because they think it quenches the Spirit's work, still follow some order. This was as true of the first Baptists who separated from Anglican formalism as it is of the new contemporary churches today who are striving not to be predictable. But given time, spontaneity always moves into formalism. People are creatures of habit and designed for structure.

Although admittedly a formal order of worship has been abused by some, let's not *das Kind mit dem Bade ausschütten,* as Martin Luther may have said in his day.[3] A formal order of worship is not something to be avoided by any church.

The Bible teaches: 'Let all things be done decently and in order.'[4] The Greek word for order is *'taxis',* the root of the English word taxonomy. It means a regular arrangement in time, a fixed succession, or an official dignity around a process. An order of worship gives us a structure to allocate time and so ensure that every necessary act of public worship is carried out on a regular basis. It also provides dignity for our worship.

There are several variations on orders of worship found within Christianity. Some churches are liturgical, meaning they use a liturgy[5] approved by a denominational body and there is little or no room for variety from church to church.

With apologies to readers from liturgical churches, my area of specialty and knowledge is limited to 'evangelical and fundamental' Bible churches. I will stick with that for the rest of the chapter.

---

2   Hippolytus, *Apostolic Tradition*, c. A.D. 215.
3   Old German proverb, translated 'Throw the baby out with the bathwater.'
4   1 Corinthians 14:40 (AV).
5   Liturgy literally means 'the work of religious service'.

The typical traditional order of service for Sunday morning might look something like this.

1.   Instrumental music before the service starts (prelude)
2.   Opening congregational hymn
3.   Brief opening prayer
4.   More congregational hymns
5.   Choir
6.   Announcements
7.   Short prayer for the offering
8.   Offering with musical accompaniment (offertory)
9.   Fellowship/greeting time
10. Another congregational hymn
11. Special music
12. Reading of the Bible passage for the sermon
13. Sermon
14. Closing congregational hymn and invitation
15. Closing prayer (benediction)
16. Instrumental music after the service (postlude)

All of this is typically packed into sixty to ninety minutes. Some churches may fit in a drama or children's message each week. On a monthly or quarterly schedule, the Lord's Supper will be inserted somewhere in this (usually at the end) and baptisms will be scheduled as needed. An innovation in the past fifty years is the use of a religious movie in place of the sermon.

Modern (or 'contemporary') services streamline this long list into something shorter like:

1. Music before the service starts
2. Worship in song (twenty-thirty minutes of continuous, flowing music)
3. Worship in giving (five minutes — with music accompaniment)
4. Worship in the Word (the sermon twenty-thirty minutes)

5. Announcements/fun (ten minutes)
6. Closing song

While the contemporary service may appear to be much shorter, simpler and less 'programed', insiders know that every second is programed very tightly. Woe to the person who misses a cue.

Is there room for improvement?

We seem to be too enamored with the 'entertainment' aspects of public worship, the components that are led by our most attractive and charismatic leaders.

1. *Music, music, and more music.* Includes congregational singing and passive listening to others performing music. Videos and dancing are often added to this segment.

2. *Preaching.* Before I comment on this, I want to affirm the absolute centrality of preaching as being vital to our public worship. The congregation needs expository preaching — and more of it! However, sadly, we have observed in some churches that this time has become a breeding ground for charismatic and entertaining story-tellers with little in the way of biblical exhortation but long on inspirational life messages. It is this specific abuse of the preaching time to which I refer.

3. *Announcements and fun time.* In some churches, this has become the devil's playground where anything goes. My old worship band played vulgar, secular rock songs as lead-ins to announcements. I have heard of a pastor who rode a motorcycle down the aisle to promote a men's conference.

I am sure the reader can provide many more examples of daftness.

These 'Big 3' aspects of public worship are given the lion's share of time, creativity and energy in our services. I see room for improvement. There are three 'missing jewels' of public worship that are often crowded out by the Big 3.

1. Prayer
2. Public reading of the Bible
3. The Lord's Supper

I hope it is proper to borrow, with much honor and respect, from the title of A. W. Tozer's classic book *Worship: The Missing Jewel*. I read this and several other Tozer books, I quote him often, and my friends and readers know that I agree with much of what he wrote about worship.

The following chapters will take a closer look at the 'missing jewels' and why they deserve more time in public worship — even if it means we should take that time away from the Big 3.

Chapter 9

The missing jewels of public worship: prayer

When it came to public worship, what did Jesus teach his disciples to do? Did he teach them to sing or play instruments or dance or put on a drama or give announcements? No. Jesus asked us to do *two* things for him when we gather together as the local church. The first was to pray in his name.[1] Then he taught us how to pray with the model of the Lord's Prayer.[2]

The Lord's Prayer	How it praises God and provides all we need
Our Father which art in heaven	He is our Father and we are his children. He is on the throne in heaven.
Hallowed be thy name	His Name is holy and must be treated as such by his worshipers.
Thy kingdom come	He is the King of Kings, the Most High Ruler of the universe. His Kingdom will come!

---

1   Matthew 18:19-20.
2   Matthew 6:9-13 (AV).

The Lord's Prayer	How it praises God and provides all we need
Thy will be done in earth, as it is in heaven	His will is perfect and all the earth is under his sovereign control.
Give us this day our daily bread	He is the Creator, Provider and Sustainer of our life.
And forgive us our debts, as we forgive our debtors	Only God can forgive our sins. When we forgive each other, we fulfill God's plan.
And lead us not into temptation, but deliver us from evil	We trust him to direct our paths and rely on him to rescue us from evil.
For thine is the kingdom, and the power, and the glory, for ever.	He is the eternal, omnipotent and Most High God.
Amen!	Yes, this is all true and I publicly testify that it is true.

Jesus taught us to pray both privately and publicly. Some will say we should not pray in public:

'And when you pray, you shall not be like the hypocrites. For they love to pray standing in the synagogues and on the corners of the streets, that they may be seen by men. But you, when you pray, go into your room, and when you have shut your door, pray to your Father.'[3]

But Jesus could not have meant to condemn all the prayers being said in the synagogues. He specifically called out the hypocrites — those who were like stage actors playing a part to win the applause of the crowd. Praying in public does not make you a hypocrite; any more than visiting a prison makes you a criminal.

---

3   Matthew 6:5-6.

However this serves as a good warning to be careful whom we ask to lead public prayers. Pastors, elders and deacons are preferred because of their biblical qualifications to lead and their experience with public prayer. Hopefully, the hypocrites did not make it into those leadership positions at your church.

When we pray, we should not rush quickly into it. We should respect this most holy of worship acts by offering our full attention. With all the activity packed into the typical worship service, there is a temptation for the leader to begin the prayer as soon as he bows his head. He ought to wait until the congregation has ceased from other activities and settled into quietness. It is amazing how fifteen seconds of silence solves this problem.

Pray for us, pastor

It is time to bring back the pastoral prayer, which has fallen into much neglect in many churches. We sheep need the shepherd of the local flock to pray for us, just as the Chief Shepherd did when he was on earth and still does for the church, interceding constantly for us in heaven as our advocate before the Father.

The early church kept the practice of pastoral prayer. 'Let the bishop pray for the people. After this let the sacrifice follow, the people standing, and praying silently.'[4]

I suspect some of our members might rebel against a five to ten minute prayer where they are forced to be silent and listen to someone else talking to God on their behalf. Let us gently come alongside those brethren and teach them to participate silently and joyfully.

It is also time for churches to put an end to the disrespect shown to public prayer. At some churches, while a pastor is praying for the sick and the unsaved — very serious matters — musicians and other 'worship leaders' are busy shuffling sheet

---

4 *Apostolic Constitutions*, Book 2, Section 7.

music, adjusting microphones, changing instrumental settings, or moving across the platform to their next performance position. The media booth personnel are frantically re-adjusting sound levels, lighting, computer presentations, or a dozen other technology items. Ushers are walking about when they should be still and hushed.

Pastors, put a stop to that immediately! If every worshiper in your service cannot pause for the prayer, then you are booking your service too tight and you need to loosen it up just a bit. Be careful that you are not more concerned about the form and flow of your worship service than you are about prayer.

Why do we bow our heads when we pray?

Bowing one's head in prayer is the last remaining fragment of *'proskuneo'* worship to be found in the vast majority of churches. Bowing my head is a sign of submission and devotion towards the one I am addressing. In ancient times, this signified surrender to a superior person and total trust in the one worshiped. At some churches, it is also the custom to drop to the knees in prayer. I think that is a good custom and we will see biblical support for it later.

Should we literally prostrate ourselves whenever we pray to God, just as our spiritual forefathers did? Some may recoil from that thought as we consider the images on our television sets of Muslims, for example, performing their prayer ritual, which includes an act of prostration. At least in its form this fits the meaning of worship when the Bible was written.

But God sees our hearts. He is not fooled by a form of prostration; he desires a humble and submissive heart that is devoted to him. We have freedom to bow while standing or sitting, to kneel, or to lay flat on our faces in our private devotions. What happens in public worship is another matter.

To raise or not to raise

'I desire therefore that the men pray everywhere, lifting up holy hands, without wrath and doubting.'[5] The apostle Paul could not have imagined the future arguments that would be caused by this simple command. Based on this one passage, some think we should all pray while looking up to God and raising our arms to heaven. Is this another example of a 'one-verse wonder,'[6] or does the Bible have ample support for the face-and hand-raisers?

What did Jesus do? He prayed all the time and there are many verses about his prayer life. The one time we hear of his physical posture is in the garden of Gethsemane. There he fell to the ground and knelt on his knees to pray.[7] The disciples asked Jesus, 'Lord, teach us to pray', and he spoke not a word about the proper physical posture.[8] This can be explained in that they already knew what to do, so there was no need for Jesus to state the obvious.

Peter knelt to pray and God raised Tabitha from the dead.[9] Paul led two prayer sessions where everyone knelt down: with the elders of Ephesus[10] and the disciples at Tyre.[11] The Greek words for prayer (noun) and praying (verb) may hold another clue. The noun *proseuche* means a prayer but it also means worship. The verb *proseuchomai* means to pray to God, to worship, to supplicate. Earlier, we learned all about the posture of worshipers, and it was certainly not upward-looking.

What does it mean to supplicate? The English word comes from the Latin for supple, which means capable of being bent or folded, able to perform bending movements with ease. The

---

5   1 Timothy 2:8.
6   The practice of establishing a doctrine based on one verse.
7   Matthew 26:39; Mark 14:35; Luke 22:41.
8   Luke 11:1.
9   Acts 9:40.
10   Acts 20:36.
11   Acts 21:5.

89

evidence here would seem to be in favor of kneeling and bowing for prayer, and against standing and looking up and raising hands skyward. Those who disagree must not cause dissension in public worship.

Amen!

Did you know Jesus said 'Amen' at least 103 times in the Gospels?[12] But he never once said Amen at the end of his prayers. Are you shocked to learn that? Then why do we say 'Amen' at the end of all our prayers?

Amen is a Hebrew word that made its way into Greek and straight into English and other languages. It was the word chosen by the Holy Spirit for what Jesus spoke and meant.

The Hebrew word origins for Amen are interesting: sure; faithful; true; firm; certain. The AV translation of Amen is 'verily', as in one of Jesus' well-known phrases, 'verily, I say unto you'. Another rendering is 'I tell you the truth'. Jesus said 'Amen' at the beginning of his statements, not at the end. He was signaling that the point he was about to make was true, certain and permanent.

Jesus was speaking the will of God the Father, and Amen was his opening statement. When the one called the Truth states he is telling you the truth, then you should pay close attention and believe what he says next! In the Gospel of John God wanted to make sure we understood this by having Jesus say it twice — verily, verily.

Now, it is very interesting that Jesus is the only person recorded in the four Gospels to say the word 'Amen'. That makes sense, as he was the one speaking the truth to us while he was on earth. Jesus did not end his own prayers with Amen. Again that makes sense — the Lord could not pray that his own will might

---

12   In the Authorized Version.

be done, or his own promise fulfilled. Finally, Jesus himself is called the Amen.[13]

Who uses Amen at the *end* of a prayer? His followers do. Jesus taught us to do this in the Lord's Prayer. We are not to say 'I am about to tell you the truth' at the beginning of our prayers, as if we had some truth of our own to utter. It is only at the end that we affirm the truth of what has been prayed — who God is and what Jesus has done! We are witnessing to God's truth with every Amen. Our Amen is the 'so be it' because the truth will never change.

There are no Amens found in the entire book of Acts. The next Amens are from Paul, who was inspired to use Amen many times to end his doxologies, prayers and benedictions.[14] We are also taught by Paul to use Amen when someone else finishes a prayer, as a sign that we understood what they said, we affirm it to be true, and it has built us up in the faith.[15]

Peter uses Amen several times[16] and Jude completes his short letter with the Amen.[17] John says Amen early in Revelation[18] before Amens are offered in heaven at the end of praises to God and Jesus. Fittingly, the last word of the Bible is Amen!

Summary

Prayer is the number one missing jewel in our worship services. Prayer is the primary act of Christian worship and praise. A prayer is the purest way for anyone to bring words of praise to

---

13   Revelation 3:14.

14   There are many examples of Paul's use of Amen at the end of a prayer, benediction or doxology. Romans 1:25; Romans 9:5; Romans 11:36; Romans 15:33; Romans 16:20; Romans 16:24; Romans 16:27; 2 Corinthians 1:20; Galatians 1:5; Galatians 6:18; Ephesians 3:21; Philippians 4:20; 1 Thessalonians 5:28; 1 Timothy 1:17; 1 Timothy 6:16; 2 Timothy 4:18; Titus 3:15; Hebrews 13:21.

15   1 Corinthians 14:16-17.

16   1 Peter 4:11; 1 Peter 5:11; 1 Peter 5:14; 2 Peter 3:18.

17   Jude 1:25.

18   Revelation 1:6-7.

God. The words we bring to God are far more important than any music that accompanies them.

How much time does your church spend in prayer during its weekly service? How can your church creatively increase the time spent in prayer? If you give it five minutes now, can you double that to ten? The specific amount of time is less important than the time you give it in proportion to the other components in your worship service.

Chapter 10

The missing jewels of public worship: public reading of the Bible

I once believed that music produced the sweetest sounds to be heard in the Christian assembly. Now I know the sweetest sound is that of many pages rustling, as saints turn to the Bible passage we are about to read together. What could be closer to the heart of God than his people opening his Word?

When I am invited to speak at a local church, the host typically asks me if I would like to perform special music or lead the singing. I reply, 'No thanks, but can I lead a responsive Bible reading?' I can't wait to hear that sweet, sweet sound of pages rustling.

Reading the Bible aloud to an assembly of believers is a long-time component of public worship. Yet some Christian churches have virtually abandoned the practice or shortened it to a few verses spoken with haste. Should we be too concerned? To answer that, let's look closely at the case for public Bible reading.

Public reading is fundamental

The Law and Prophets were read weekly in every synagogue service.

- 'For Moses has had throughout many generations those who preach him in every city, being read in the synagogues every Sabbath.'[1]
- '... the voices of the Prophets which are read every Sabbath...'[2]

Jesus read the Scriptures in the synagogue, before he preached and explained what he had just read.

- 'And as His custom was, He went into the synagogue on the Sabbath day, and stood up to read. And He was handed the book of the prophet Isaiah.'[3]

In these examples, clearly the reader was doing more than just reading to himself. The context teaches that the Scriptures were read aloud to the assembled people of God. Whenever the New Testament says someone read the Scriptures, this is usually the meaning. Matthew Henry offers more insight into this weekly Sabbath practice.

> They had in their synagogues seven readers every Sabbath, the first a priest, the second a Levite, and the other five Israelites of that synagogue. We often find Christ preaching in other synagogues, but never reading, except in this synagogue at Nazareth of which he had been many years a member. Now he offered his service as he had perhaps often done; he read one of the lessons out of the prophets.

---

1   Acts 15:21.
2   Acts 13:27.
3   Luke 4:16-17a.

Note: The reading of the scripture is very proper work to be done in religious assemblies; and Christ himself did not think it any disparagement to him to be employed in it.[4]

The New Testament church read letters from the apostles to the gathered saints.

- '...they came to Antioch; and when they had gathered the multitude together, they delivered the letter. When they had read it, they rejoiced over its encouragement.'[5]
- 'I charge you by the Lord that this epistle be read to all the holy brethren.'[6]
- 'Now when this epistle is read among you, see that it is read also in the church of the Laodiceans, and that you likewise read the epistle from Laodicea.'[7]
- 'By which, when you read, you may understand my knowledge in the mystery of Christ.'[8]
- 'Till I come, give attention to reading, to exhortation, to doctrine.'[9]

The early church (from the second to the fourth centuries) also read the Scriptures aloud in their weekly meeting. Here are two reports about the practice from letters written by Church Fathers.

And on the day called Sunday, all who live in cities or in the country gather together to one place, and the memoirs of the apostles or the writings of the prophets are read, as long as time permits; then, when the reader has ceased, the

---

4   Matthew Henry *Commentary* on Luke 4:16.
5   Acts 15:30-31.
6   1 Thessalonians 5:27.
7   Colossians 4:16.
8   Ephesians 3:4.
9   Probably the public reading of the Scriptures, though surely private reading is not to be excluded. Robertson's Word Pictures.

president verbally instructs, and exhorts to the imitation of these good things.[10]

Let the reader stand upon some high place: let him read the books of Moses, of Joshua the son of Nun, of the Judges, and of the Kings and of the Chronicles, and those written after the return from the captivity; and besides these, the books of Job and of Solomon, and of the sixteen prophets.

Afterwards let our Acts be read, and the Epistles of Paul our fellow-worker, which he sent to the churches under the conduct of the Holy Spirit; and afterwards let a deacon or a presbyter read the Gospels, both those which Matthew and John have delivered to you, and those which the fellow-workers of Paul received and left to you, Luke and Mark.

And while the Gospel is read, let all the presbyters and deacons, and all the people, stand up in great silence...[11]

Liturgies of the Word

In the centuries since, churches have devoted a good portion of the worship service to the public reading of the Bible. Here is a brief overview of different worship traditions and how they treat this. Please note it is not my intention here to endorse any or all of these. I wish only to show that public reading is an important component of God's public worship, no matter the denomination or sect.

The Divine Liturgy is the common term for the service used in the Eastern Orthodox and Eastern Catholic churches. Based on first-century traditions, the first part is the Liturgy of the Word and includes reading of scriptures and the sermon.

---

10 Justin Martyr's *First Apology*, Chapter LXVII — Weekly worship of the Christians.
11 *Apostolic Constitutions*, Book 2, Section 7. Circa 4th century.

The Mass is the Roman Catholic Church service. It has a section titled 'The Liturgy of the Word'. On Sundays, three Scripture readings are given. The first is from the Old Testament or, during Easter season, the Acts of the Apostles. The second reading is from the New Testament. The final reading is the proclamation of the Gospels.

The Divine Service of the Lutheran Church dates from Martin Luther's changes to the Latin Mass in 1523. It has a section titled 'The Service of the Word'. The First Lesson or Old Testament reading usually relates to the Gospel lesson for the day. The Epistle is taken from the letters of the Apostles. The Gospel is read or chanted by the pastor. The congregation rise at the singing of the Alleluia and remain standing while the Gospel is read.

The Book of Common Prayer, dating to 1549, guides the Anglican Church worship service. It specifies the Epistle and Gospel readings for the Sunday Communion Service. Old Testament and New Testament readings for daily prayer are included, as well as Psalm readings.

The Directory of Public Worship is a manual for the Presbyterian Church. The Westminster Assembly of Divines was appointed in 1643 to restructure the Church of England and in the process produced the major confessional documents of the Presbyterian faith, including the *Directory of Public Worship*. The entire worship service is centered on the reading of Scripture. The scriptures are read in order, a chapter from each testament at a time.

The oldest records of *Baptist* worship from 1607-1609 show that regular public reading of the Bible was prominent even for the anti-liturgical Separatists:

The order of the worship and government of our church is we begin with a prayer, after read [sic] some one or two chapters of the Bible, give the sense thereof, and confer upon the same, that done we lay aside our books.

No apocrypha must be brought into the public assemblies, for there only God's word and the lively voice of His own grace must be heard in the public assemblies.[12]

I grew up in a Methodist church. The responsive reading was a regular feature of the worship service. Most hymnals still have a section of Scripture readings formatted for this antiphonal, call-response type of reading. In many independent Bible churches, the custom is for someone to read aloud the text for the pastor's sermon before he preaches from it. This is an old tradition worth keeping.

Can't everyone read it themselves?

In past centuries, most church members could not read or did not possess a personal Bible, so the spoken Word in church was their only option. Today Christians in most countries have a very high literacy rate and several Bibles to choose from, and they can simply read the Bible to themselves in or out of church. It could be argued that the need for public reading has passed into history.

But there is something special, powerful and God-ordained about the *spoken* Word. Hearing the gospel is the method for conversion prescribed in the Bible. 'And how shall they believe in Him whom they have not heard? ... So then faith comes by hearing, and hearing by the word of God.'[13]

And how shall they hear without a preacher? God ordained that his Word should be transmitted not only from the written page to the eyes, but also from the mouth of a person to the ears of another. Audio versions of the Bible are very popular

---

12 Letter from Hughe Bromhead, member of John Smyth's congregation. From *History of the Free Churchmen called the Brownists, Pilgrim Fathers and Baptists in the Dutch republic 1581-1701* by J. G. de Hoop Scheffer.
13 Romans 10:14,17.

today for personal use, proving the effectiveness of the spoken Word.

More Bible, less life message?

We could use more of God's Word in the content coming from our pulpits. We already have enough 'words of men' to go around. While there are many benefits when good preachers and teachers expound and apply the Bible to life, their words alone simply cannot match the wonderful and miraculous power of the words of Scripture. Look at the great things the Word alone can do for us:

- The church is cleansed.[14]
- We are sanctified.[15]
- It is our weapon for spiritual warfare.[16]
- We are instructed.[17]
- We are admonished.[18]
- Our hearts are judged.[19]
- We are rebuked.[20]
- We are encouraged.[21]
- We are made strong.[22]
- We will overcome the wicked one.[23]

This reminds us that Scripture is of the utmost importance for salvation, sanctification and life. Words of men simply

---

14 Ephesians 5:26.
15 John 17:17; Ephesians 5:26.
16 Ephesians 6:17.
17 *Ibid.*
18 Colossians 3:16.
19 Hebrews 4:12.
20 2 Timothy 4:2.
21 *Ibid.*
22 1 John 2:14.
23 *Ibid.*

cannot substitute for the powerful Word of God spoken aloud to his people.

Handle with care

The public reading of the Bible should be taken seriously and treated with the respect it clearly deserves. If you wish to 'kill' any enthusiasm for it, then treat it casually as if it were only a 'filler' between great music performances. Or assume the congregation is bored by it and try to spice it up.

Here are some common mistakes I have observed in worship services, that are guaranteed to ruin this great tradition:

1. Announce the passage you will read aloud, ask everyone to turn to it in their Bibles, and then start reading it immediately before anyone else has found it. This is very rude to the congregation. It also shows that the speaker is in a hurry to get through it.

No! The only proper way to do this is to wait until the rustling of pages has stopped completely. I like to tell the congregation that 'I won't start reading aloud until the rustling of pages has stopped, so we go as fast as the slowest page turner.' At first they chuckle nervously. Will we be here until Slow Old Elmer catches up? What about our lunch reservations at noon? Then it sinks in: this is God's Word and we can take the time to respect it. God's people will recognize this, even when the pastor or worship leader has little faith in them.

2. Read aloud in a voice and tone as if you are reading the phonebook or a legal brief. Do not give it the same energy and passion as you give the music. Drone on, acting like you are a child in school again who only cares to get through the boring lesson. Do not train your readers, just let them stand up there and 'wing' it.

No! We should read the Bible aloud with conviction, confidence, soberness, joy and excitement as the text itself allows. Read authentically from your own faith and love for the Word. Do not read dramatically as if an actor reading Shakespeare. This is not a play and you are not an actor. God's Word does not need that much help to work on the hearts of the listener.

Consider also a responsive reading, which takes the burden off one single reader and allows the congregation a 50% share of the task.

3. Ignore the hard of hearing and deaf brethren, or those for whom English is not their first language. Do not use a person who knows sign language. Do not ask the congregation to open their Bibles and read along. If you use a screen, don't project the words there.

No! We should always work hard to ensure everyone present can participate. To accomplish this requires only one tenth of the energy and creativity that goes into the music.

4. During the reading, allow other pastors, or the musicians, or the ushers, to perform other duties. Send the signal to everyone that attention to Bible reading is optional for some.

God forbid! Pastors, make it clear that while God's Word is read aloud, everyone should attend to it.

Summary

There is a very strong case for all Christian churches to devote more time for public reading of the Bible. How much time does your worship service devote to this? I will not tell you how many minutes are acceptable because it is a matter of proportion and balance. The important thing is to make sure we don't neglect it because we crowd it out with the Big 3 of music, preaching, and announcements/fun.

If you don't think you can expand your service time to fit in a good, long Bible reading, one easy place where you can find the time is to sing one less song. Unless you are singing the actual words of Scripture in all those songs (as some congregations do well), then you are filling space with more 'words of men' that may be very comforting but have no real power like the Word of God.

We call ourselves 'people of the Word'. Then let us prove it with our public acts.

Chapter 11

The missing jewels of public worship:
the Lord's Supper

When it comes to public worship, Jesus asked us to do two things for him when we gather together as the local church. The first was to pray in his name. We covered that in a previous chapter. His second command for public worship? Proclaim the Lord's death till he comes.[1] This is the Lord's Supper — also called the Lord's Table, Communion or the Eucharist.

This chapter will deal with independent Bible churches that face issues of timing and neglect of this second and incredibly vital request from Jesus. It is not intended as a theological discussion of sacraments versus ordinance, and the other serious issues that divide us over this sacred act of worship.

I am a member of an independent Baptist church. You could call us the Remembrance churches. We are those who 'do this in *remembrance* of Him'.[2] By observing the Lord's Supper, we remember that Jesus redeemed us from sin by his suffering and death on the cross. This also reminds every generation of

---

1   1 Corinthians 11:26.
2   1 Corinthians 11:25.

new Christians about the New Covenant in Christ's blood. That should be enough for you to know where I stand on it.

How often is often?

For as often as you eat this bread and drink this cup.[3]

What did it mean by 'often'? Did Jesus and Paul mean we should observe it at every meal we eat?

I am an inductive Bible study student. When faced with such a question, the first place I look for answers is not in a commentary, lexicon, sermon or book about the question. I look first within the Bible for the answer, believing Scripture interprets Scripture and context is king. After that, I consult extra-biblical study tools and Bible teachers to make sure I am in alignment with good teaching.

Let's look first at the obvious clues found in the Bible. When Jesus instituted the Lord's Supper in the Gospels, what was he observing? He said, 'I will keep the Passover at your house with My disciples.'[4] Jesus and his disciples were celebrating Passover.

I have had the great privilege to lead a fulfilled Passover Seder meal for family and friends. Seder is the traditional Jewish celebration of Passover and, several thousand years after the Exodus, it is still miraculously observed today. A fulfilled Seder is for Messianic Jews and Christians, because Jesus is the fulfillment of the Passover lamb and he is the Messiah promised to take away the sins of the world. It is amazing to see in the Seder how Jesus fulfilled prophecies when he became the Passover Lamb.[5]

Jesus and his disciples were celebrating the Seder meal when he broke the bread and raised the cup. The cup that he

---

3   *Ibid.*
4   Matthew 26:18.
5   1 Corinthians 5:7.

called 'the new testament in my blood, which is shed for you'[6] corresponded to the third cup of the Seder meal, which is the cup of redemption. Hallelujah!

How often is Seder? Once a year. Is that what Jesus literally meant? As often as you eat the Seder bread and drink the Seder cup? Here is an argument for once a year. But it does not adequately explain what happened soon after in the New Testament church.

Let's look next into the church at Corinth who were observing the Lord's Supper only a few decades after the Lord instituted it. Some of the original disciples who were with Jesus at the Last Supper were still alive, and we can surmise they advised the churches on this very question concerning the Lord's Supper.

What was the Corinthian problem? Did they neglect the Lord's Supper for long periods of time? No; on the contrary, it appears they practiced it quite often; but they did it very badly. The apostle Paul had to write and correct their errors, in some places with a strong rebuking tone. He addresses this in 1 Corinthians 11:20-34, beginning with this attention-grabber: '*Therefore when you come together in one place, it is <u>not</u> to eat the Lord's Supper!*'

Paul is in the midst of teaching a long lesson on how to act properly when the church is assembled.[7] In their meetings, some of the Corinthians were acting like self-centered me-monsters: rowdy, worldly, carnal, vulgar, divisive, flaunting their closeness to idolatry, and very disrespectful of others. When they sat down to eat, they did not wait for others.

We are looking for clues related to time — how often. The clue here is 'when you come together in one place'; in other words, when they assembled as a church. And how often did the Corinthian church meet? In all probability, this happened

---

6   Luke 22:20 (AV).
7   1 Corinthians 11:17,18,20,33,34; 12:28; 14:19,23,26,33,34.

once a week on the Lord's Day when the church held an agape, or love, feast as part of their meeting.

The love feast was a very necessary and loving component of the early church, since most of the members were in a constant state of famine. At some point during the love feast, an elder would lead the assembled in the observance of the Lord's Supper, just as Paul explained it here. This is the argument for a weekly observance.

That is all the help we seem to get from the Bible. The rest of our information comes from writings from the early Church Fathers such as Justin Martyr and Clement of Alexandria, and from documents such as the Apostles' *Didache.* These historical documents, while not authoritative like the Bible, point to a weekly observance in the churches, which then became the tradition for many centuries to come.

Not very often

Do you know how often we observe the Lord's Supper at the typical independent Baptist or Bible church? Some do it monthly; others when a fifth Sunday falls in a month, which occurs only four times a year. Why this schedule?

When I researched it, pastors could not explain to me how this timing had anything to do with biblical guidance or respect for centuries of Christian tradition. They fell back on 'That's the way we've always done it.' Some who remembered their church history mentioned that at one time independent churches need-ed to clearly separate from the worship of Anglican and Catholic churches who had the Eucharist at the center of their services. Therefore Communion was removed from weekly services.

Others told me they thought independent churches stopped weekly Communion because they didn't want to be like those 'dead' mainline denominations. Those worshipers were accused of only going through ritualistic motions because they do it every Sunday.

Of course, the same charge of 'dead ritual' could be made against *any* weekly practice found in independent church services — and it has been. The contemporary church growth movement is built on selling the snake oil that traditional independent services are 'dead' and the people there are just hypocrites going through the motions. Ouch!

The irregular observance of the Lord's Supper practiced in most independent Bible churches is also found in the contemporary mega-churches. This is no surprise, as many sprung out of the same independent and fundamental Bible churches they criticized.

How often is often enough? Why not weekly? I think independent churches have long ago made their point. No one would suspect us of 'mindless ritual' if we returned to a more frequent schedule of observance.

The other problem of neglect

When Remembrance churches do observe the Lord's Supper, we have to be very careful that we do not tack it on at the end of a regular service schedule and hurry through it. I have seen this done too many times in my journey, and it is regrettable.

Before the Lord's Supper begins, we solemnly encourage every partaker to examine himself so he does not come to the table of the Lord in an unworthy manner.[8] The Greek word for unworthy is *anaxios*, meaning to come irreverently, without any reverence or godly fear, and acting in a way that is not suitable to the serious occasion — in other words, acting like the Corinthians. The punishment for unworthy eating and drinking is sickness and even death.[9]

---

8   1 Corinthians 11:28-29.
9   1 Corinthians 11:30.

This is a vital preparation time for us to confess our sins and put aside all joking and the party-spirit and get down to serious business. But when we place the ceremony at the end of the service, how distracted are the partakers after seventy to eighty minutes of a morning service and with the ending just ahead? What about those with small children, or the elderly, who may have difficulty concentrating at this point?

We do this vital act of worship a great disservice when we treat it that way. Some churches have changed their practice from an occasional observance tacked on to the end, to a weekly observance placed before the sermon. This has more than one benefit.

Pastors who have made this change have remarked on the difference they have noticed in preaching to a receptive congregation who have been engaged in fervent prayer, have confessed their sins, and have been reconciled with their brethren.

Summary

Jesus asked us to do this for him until he comes again, and to do it often. How often does your church observe the Lord's Supper? Is it an 'add-on' at the end of your service? Do you treat it with the utmost of respect in every way?

I am calling for a serious re-examination of this practice among our churches. Let each man be fully convinced in his own mind.

Part II

Wrong turns and cul-de-sacs

Chapter 12

The last worship leader

Once upon a time, there was a person on the church leadership team who was in charge of the music during the services. We called that person 'the minister of music' or a very similar title.

He or she was a trained musician with a sacred and/or classical music background. The main responsibilities were to select the music for the service, lead the congregational singing, conduct the choir, and manage the special music ministry. Sometimes this person was also the organist or pianist and led the singing from the keyboard. In smaller churches, volunteers filled the same roles.

Something changed in the past forty years. With the onset of Contemporary Christian Music (CCM) in the early 1970s, a few churches began to add a 'contemporary' service for young people. This service was distinctive for the use of a rock-style band playing songs in a pop/rock musical style and with a front-man for the band. The modern worship leader was born.

From the 1970s into the 1980s, Pentecostal churches adopted this style of service. Rock music's repetition and driving backbeat, used frequently in the secular realm to enhance trance states for drug users 'tripping out' to the music, was the perfect enhancement to their ecstatic, emotional style of worship.

From the late 1980s, the church growth movement adopted this worship-music experience, toned it down, and made it the centerpiece of how to build a large church. Rick Warren, pastor of Saddleback Church (over 20,000 members) and the leader of the Purpose-Driven Church growth industry, famously said that when he started Saddleback he *underestimated* the power of music, and if he had to start his church over again, he would put more effort into the music program. He also taught that the music should be whatever is current with the culture, and specifically pop-rock.

With this newly discovered power of music to grow churches instantly and to transport members spiritually into a 'better' worship experience, it would no longer be enough for us to have a mere music minister or song leader. Those titles smacked of the old traditionalism many were keen to leave behind as quickly as possible. Now the modern worship leader took center stage.

Who's really in charge?

'I hate to put it this way, but the worship guy has to have as much clout as the lead pastor does. That's how important music is on Sunday.' Michael W. Smith believes a church's senior pastor sometimes has too much authority when it comes to the worship part of church services. 'That's my opinion; I could be wrong.'[1]

We should credit Smith with some honesty, for exposing in public a belief that most worship leaders would rather keep to themselves. But Smith has not acted as if he had any doubts about whether his opinion was right or wrong. He moved full-

---

1   Interview in *Charisma* magazine, 2003.

speed ahead, as a firm believer and fervent promoter that 'new' worship music is the key to effective Christian worship.

Should we expect anything less than a biased view from a man who is a professional musician? His worship albums are top sellers. One can hardly expect Smith or any other musician to downplay the role of music in worship. They are hopelessly in love with the music and derive income from it.

But his viewpoint is typical of the worship leader movement and adequately sums up what is wrong with modern worship — it's *all about the music*. When you attend the typical modern worship service (in person or over the Internet), it is plain to see. Some of the other biblical worship components may be present but no doubt is left that you are attending a well-produced music concert and that the vast majority of time and energy has gone into the musical performance.

Could Smith and the modern worship movement possibly be wrong on elevating music to such a position? Based on what we've learned about worship in the previous chapters, the answer is yes. We can clearly state that worship is *not* about the music! Music should play a far lesser role than they give it.

Time for a change?

What further need, then, do we have for musicians masquerading as biblical worship leaders? I am calling for an end to the man-made and unbiblical experiment called the modern worship leader. Allow me to summarize the reasons.

1. *Worship is far more than music.*

Music has its proper place in public worship. But placing a musician in charge of worship distorts that balance and we end up with too much music, which leads to neglect of the other vital components of worship.

The modern worship leader movement recognizes this problem too. Seminars, blogs and books tell worship leaders to seek balance and not to focus only on music. But those are small voices trying to be heard over the din of music, music, and more music. Passionate musicians are hardly able to reform themselves. The vast majority of worship leader material is still concerned with selecting songs, writing songs, managing songs, musical performance techniques, training a band, promoting music on a website, new music technologies etc.

If a person is a musician and leads music at a church, then we should call them the song leader, the minister in music, the accompanist, or simply the brother who is skilled at music and can help the rest of us along. We should end the worship confusion in our churches by ending the title of worship leader.

2. *There are no worship leaders in the Bible.*

Surely something as important as the worship leader would have been mentioned many times in the Bible, plainly and with several closely aligned references. But it is not. While some will argue from silence whenever it suits their case, I urge you to think on this.

There is a song leader named Chenaniah found in 1 Chronicles.[2] But he was hardly a good role model for today's worship leader. Chenaniah was the master singer of the Levites and his job was more like a chief monk who led the choir at a monastery. He and his musicians were a small group with musical skills, carefully chosen from among the priestly tribe of Levites. They were purified for temple service and not to be defiled by the affairs of the world.

They were the only musicians permitted to perform the sacred music for the Jewish worship service at the tabernacle and later the temple. No one else sang or played instruments, except them. Only Levites were allowed to lead the divine

---

2   1 Chronicles 15:22.

worship of the Jews; even the kings dared not interfere.[3] King David, the patron saint of some modern worship leaders, was *not* a worship leader.

Jesus is the most important person to consult. He gave us the list of leaders to equip the church. Here are the Spirit-ordained roles from Christ: 'And He Himself gave some to be apostles, some prophets, some evangelists, and some pastors and teachers.'[4]

In the New Testament, Paul, Peter and John are completely silent about worship leaders. They had ample opportunity to add worship leader to the lists of offices and gifts, but were not inspired to do so.

There is no mention of a worship leader for the church. Nor is there support for the so-called 'lead worshiper' role as some have tried to reposition the worship leader. But this should be expected. Why would Jesus need a worship leader for his churches, since he became our High Priest and is ministering on our behalf in the heavenly sanctuary? Christ is our worship leader, the only one we really need.

At one of my seminars, a clever person challenged my argument by pointing out that we can't find the phrase 'Sunday school' in the Bible yet we have Sunday school teachers and superintendents. He chose a poor argument. The New Testament has much to say about teachers in the church and there is a Christ-ordained office of teacher. Whether they teach the Bible on Sundays or Tuesdays or whatever day does not matter.

The same cannot be said of worship leaders. We should not force the Scriptures to support the office of worship leader.

3. *The worship leader movement is corrupted by fame.*

You may think your worship leader is just a humble servant who wants nothing but to serve the church. But through his

---

3   2 Chronicles 26:16.
4   Ephesians 4:11.

Internet contacts with new worship songs, artists and seminars, he inevitably becomes part of a very aggressive music industry that encourages worship leaders to seek personal fame and sell worship for a profit.

Success is no longer measured by the old terms, that is, one's faithfulness in serving the local church. Now success is about writing your own songs, cutting your own worship CDs, and promoting yourself and your worship band on Facebook. This siren call is very hard to resist. I have counseled dozens of young worship leaders who were unaware this was taking over until they were under the influence.

The praise that people throw at the feet of worship leaders is nauseating. To illustrate what I mean, *Worship Leader* magazine lets their readers vote each year for award-winners in categories such as Best Praise and Worship Song; Best Worship Project; Best Scripture Song; and Breakthrough Artist.

This kind of thing may seem perfectly harmless; but is it? Is it helpful to the fans to concentrate their thoughts in this way on the performance of the artists? Is it helpful to the artists themselves to be the center of this kind of attention?

Acknowledging the very problem I have raised, *Worship Leader* magazine tries to take the moral high ground. They claim the awards are not 'a popularity contest that glorifies celebrity',[5] but this seems to me to be ingenious rather than ingenuous.

One is tempted to ask, 'How many shouts of "Praise the Lord" does it take to balance out one Best Worship Project award?' When the awards are handed out, does the obligatory 'It's not about me, it's about God' truly give to God the unshared glory he rightfully deserves?

The question that we should all be asking is: what percentage of praise and honor is God willing to share with a worship leader? The answer may be found in this passage:

---

5   2009 Worship Leader Readers' Choice Awards, worshipleader.com

I am the LORD; that is my name! I will not give my glory to another or my praise to idols.[6]

I know some will accuse me of throwing out the baby with the bathwater. Not all worship leaders can be tarred with this brush, they will say, and it is not fair to criticize everyone because of the excesses of the few. But this infection has spread far deeper and wider than the few. I see no other cure than to cut out all the tumors, malignant and benign, in the hope of saving the patient.

Not a personal grudge

I spent several years as a worship leader, and through my books and speaking ministry I am in communication with worship leaders from across the globe and across different Christian groups. I think I understand the heart and motivation of the modern worship leader.

They are passionate about leading God's people in worship and really sincere about it. These are well-meaning Christians with some musical talent, although frankly some are second-rate pop musicians. I have nothing against them as Christians and pray they will grow in grace and the knowledge of Christ.

I simply think that based on the evidence, worship leaders are wasting their time in a worthless pursuit without biblical support, a vanity play that is misleading Christ's church into a very worldly form of worship. Look at the church today — where are the most desperate needs for people to serve? Do we need more music?

Get real! We already have an entire generation of Christians standing in line who think they could be the next American Idol, or believe they too can be a worship leader because they mastered one of those silly guitar praise and worship video games.

---

6   Isaiah 42:8 (NIV).

Decision time

If you are a worship leader, stop doing it now. Take some time off from being on the platform every week running the 'god' show. Musical talent is not a spiritual gift. When you are off the 'Sunday to Sunday' treadmill, you can find out the true spiritual gift(s) God has given you. If you have the gift to teach the Bible in small groups, get busy on it because that is badly needed in every church.

Maybe you have the gift of mercy but because you spend all your time working on being a great worship leader (and it does consume you), there was never time to visit those in your church who could use your help. Take all that passion and energy and sincerity you are wasting on an unnecessary service and ask God to help you channel it into a service that will equip the saints.

If you think you should stick with music, you may end up back in that old traditional role called the 'song leader'. No more mystical, magical pixie-dust worship talk; just you, a hymnal, an accompanist and the congregation, together offering the sacrifice of praise to God in the time-honored tradition.

The last worship leader?

I think the evidence is clear and strong that we should stop this experiment. Pastors and elders will need to be convinced of this, since they are the ones who approved the worship leader in our churches, and they are the ones who can change it.

When the last worship leader leaves, some will worry about who will lead our worship services. Fear not. We already have that leader in our churches. His name is the senior pastor, and for twenty centuries since Christ we have entrusted this vital role to sober and godly men.

But what about the 'worship pastor', a fairly recent innovation? Some Christian colleges and seminaries offer worship pastor programs, an expansion of the traditional minister of music role and a recognition of the popularity of the worship leader movement. But for the same reasons already given in this book, the church does not need this special title.

Chapter 13

Fakery on a massive scale, masquerading as authenticity

The worship pastor at a large church in America announced that while enjoying the season finale of *American Idol* he came up with three important lessons for worship leaders, the first of which was 'authenticity counts'.[1]

One hardly knows whether to laugh or cry. How can there be anything approaching authenticity in such a show? He was referring to the grand finale concert, *not* the local auditions where someone stands in front of judges and sings a cappella.[2] In this made-for-TV program, all the modern tricks of camera angles, audio techniques, make-up artists, wardrobe consultants, image consultants and faked music were given their full rein. Yet this Christian leader still found it 'authentic' enough to be an example to worship leaders. Why?

Authenticity is a very important buzz-word for contemporary Christian worshipers. They crave an authentic experience with God. They also believe they can always spot a religious hypocrite, which is the polar opposite of the authentic worshiper.

---

1   'American Idol: Three Lessons for Worship Leaders', Integrity Music web site, May 2005.
2   A song performed without instrumental accompaniment.

Yet in their search for a total body, soul and spirit worship experience that is authentic, many have been fooled by entertainment fakery. What is fake has become authentic to them. The price tags were switched, so that what is truly authentic has become despised, rejected or ignored by them.

There is nothing wrong with looking for the authentic in Christian practice. Authentic simply means genuine; real; not false or copied; as in 'an authentic antique'. Jesus Christ is authentic. The Bible is authentic. The love of Christian brethren is genuine. Outside of that, there is a world built on fakery masquerading as authenticity, lying in wait to trap us in a web of lies, vanity, sensuality and immorality.

> And no wonder, for Satan himself masquerades as an angel of light. It is not surprising, then, if his servants masquerade as servants of righteousness.[3]

Now more than ever, Christians need the ability to distinguish between the genuine and the fake. We live in perilous times for the seeker of authenticity. Are Christians ready to discern the difference?

The age of digital prestidigitation

With special software, any photo — past or present — can be altered. Some uses are fairly benign and useful — for example, removing the red-eye from a family portrait. But the same software can place into a photo a person who was never actually there and so can easily fool others. This is happening every minute now on the Internet.

There is no such thing as 'reality' TV, yet some Christians (even worship leaders such as the fellow above) are avid followers

---

3   2 Corinthians 11:14-15a (NIV).

of the shows. When you put humans in front of a TV camera, their behavior is altered by the mere presence of that camera. There is always a script and a producer to bend reality into the desired storyline. The ultimate goal is to entertain viewers while making the actors look their very best, or worst if the script calls for it.

The cameras are fed into a computer where all kinds of fakery can be added before you see it on your TV. And that TV news personality that you trust? That is an actor who has trained very hard to look and sound 'trusted' and knows how to use the camera to create trust.

Moving closer to our concern about music fakery, have you heard of Auto-Tune software? Auto-Tune corrects intonation problems in vocals or solo instruments, in real time, without distortion, while preserving all of the expressive nuance of the original performance — with audio quality so pristine that the only difference between what goes in and what comes out is the intonation.[4]

Let me translate that into what is actually going on here. Auto-Tune corrects off-pitch musical performances in real time and can make a poor or average performer sound perfect.

One prominent music critic called Auto-Tune a 'particularly sinister invention that has been putting extra shine on pop vocals since the 1990s. Essentially, it takes a poorly sung note and transposes it, placing it dead centre of where it was meant to be.'[5]

According to several online sources, auto-pitch technology has been used on thousands of music recordings since the 1990s and has become so advanced that musicians are now using it for live performances. Bloggers have talked about its use in Contemporary Christian Music for years but it is very hard to find an artist who will admit to it, for obvious reasons I would

---

4   www.antarestech.com
5   Neil McCormick, music critic of *The Daily Telegraph*, London, October 13, 2004.

think. If fakery is deemed 'sinister' for secular music use, how much worse is it when used for worship music?

Animal spirits or Holy Spirit?

Several years ago a Christian group known for their catchy pop/rock music put out an a cappella CD that literally stunned and delighted the Christian market with its beautiful vocal arrangements of great hymns. We attended their concert at a local church and during the first half of the concert, I felt rapturous from the beautiful and full vocal sounds. During the performance, the hair literally stood up on the back of my neck as I 'felt' the presence of God (or so I presumed).

At the intermission, I walked over to the sound booth to chat with the group's audio engineer and compliment him on the 'awesome' music we were experiencing. He was swapping tapes in the console and that made me very curious to find out why. His reply shocked me. The tapes were used during the a cappella performance to enhance the live vocals. We were not hearing 'authentic' vocals.

He said they did this because the CD was mixed in the recording studio to greatly enhance the vocals by layering the voices of each singer and adding reverb. When they were 'live' in concert, they felt the audience would expect that same experience.

At the end of the concert, the group sang one song without the background tape, and they sounded flat and nasal. I understood then why they needed to 'fake' the rest of the concert!

There was a disturbing dishonesty at work here. We were all misled; the worship experience was not genuine, it was manufactured by audio engineering. John Blanchard once remarked: 'There is a crucial difference between being worked up by animal spirits and being anointed by the Holy Spirit.'[6] Which spirit was at work here?

There is simply no room at all for any fakery in our worship to God. Two issues are at stake. The first is the honor we owe to God not to use 'insincere' methods to praise and serve him. The second is far more insidious: fakery creates a false spiritual experience masquerading as the Holy Spirit's work.

Why are some worship leaders so easily fooled?

Too many worship leaders and famous worship musicians borrow much of their musical inspiration and influences from wicked entertainers.[7] By giving honor and devotion to such people, the Christian musician inevitably becomes like them, adopting their tastes and tolerances. This can dull his senses, to the point where he can no longer distinguish what is authentic from what is fake.

But shouldn't anyone in charge of worship to Holy God be doing just the opposite, and fleeing musical influences filled with idolatry and evil? The only way to purify our worship is for our leaders and each one of us to avoid the seduction of the 'great god Entertainment', as A.W. Tozer called the corrupting influence of movies, TV programs and pop music.

> For centuries the Church stood solidly against every form of worldly entertainment, recognizing it for what it was. For this she was abused roundly by the sons of this world. But of late she has become tired of the abuse and has given over the struggle ... if she cannot conquer the great god Entertainment, she may as well join forces with him and make whatever use she can of his powers.[8]

---

6   *Can We Rock the Gospel*, p.146.
7   Documented extensively in *Can We Rock the Gospel* and also openly admitted in online interviews, Facebook walls and websites far too numerous to mention here.
8   Tozer on *Worship and Entertainment*, p.112.

There are also many worship leaders who have no scruples when it comes to using music and multi-media technologies to enhance the audio and visual experience in a worship service, in an effort to create a mood for worship. This is as wrong today as it was when Tozer wrote about the same worship enhancements used by high church traditionalists:

> The Presence of God in our midst — bringing a sense of Godly fear and reverence — this is largely missing today. You cannot induce it by soft organ music or light streaming through beautifully designed windows. What people feel in the presence of that kind of paganism is not the true fear of God. It is just the inducement of a superstitious dread.[9]

Modern techniques such as synthesized angel voices or echoes can produce intense feelings in listeners, masquerading as the genuine work of the Spirit. This can manufacture a sense of the presence of something 'spiritual', which is then mistaken for God.

Can you think of anything more disgusting to God? This borders on idolatry and reminds us of the pagan practice of using trance music to summon the presence of demons. The God of the Bible cannot be summoned to appear in our presence by any music or musical enhancement.[10]

Confessions of fakery on a massive scale

If you still think fakery is not a major problem with modern worship, consider the following facts from those involved in Christian music and arts.

---

9   Tozer, *Whatever Happened to Worship*, p.33.
10   Some have argued from 2 Chronicles 5:13 that God's presence can be invoked by music. But how can that interpretation be taken seriously? It violates the context of the dedication of Solomon's temple, conveniently ignores that this was a unique event never to be repeated again, and seems completely out of line with the book of Hebrews.

A CCM star participated in a cover photo shoot for *CCM Magazine*. After hours of makeup and hair styling, followed by more hours of posing for pictures, then capped off by digital photo manipulation to remove any blemishes, the magazine had its perfect 'glamor' shot for the cover. This sort of thing is standard for the CCM industry. But what happened next was not.

The star later experienced remorse at her false image on that magazine cover. She wrote a devastating article that uncovered the cynical manipulation of 'authenticity' practiced within the Christian music industry. 'Being *real* these days has become a marketing ploy,' she said. 'We are packaging that music in a way that points to ... well ... us. It's all about self, self, self.'[11] *CCM Magazine*, never one to miss out on the opportunity to peddle more 'authenticity,' published her article.

The former art director of *CCM Magazine* lifted the veil even more and gave us additional insight into the worldly star-making machinery behind the popular worship leaders. First he tells how his vision of creating an image for Chris Tomlin clashed with Tomlin's image consultants:

> Because Chris is a worship leader, he's so used to being transparent to his audience. I wanted to be sensitive to that and show a faceless image of him, where he's almost bowing in submission. As soon as his management saw the photos, they were like, 'What? Chris is not a cowboy! This is not what his image is about!'
>
> After the photo went to print, Chris' manager said, 'You know, I had a lot of resistance about this concept, but when I saw this image, it made me cry.' It was really fulfilling to hear that from someone who was that invested in imaging their artist...[12]

---

11   Nichole Nordeman, 'Skin Deep: Image & Authenticity', *CCM Magazine,* April 2007.
12   Kevin McNeese, 'Finding A Kingdom Building Passion Through Art', January 11, 2010, at NewsReleaseTuesday.com

Are you surprised at all to learn that the 'number one' worship leader and worship song writer today, the supposedly authentic and humble man who says he only wants God to receive the glory, uses *image consultants?* Why in the world would he need to have his image 'managed'? By the way, image management is a code word that really means 'make sure people only see the images we want them to see so we can maintain his popular image'. There can be only one possible reason for all of this: to sell more Chris Tomlin products.

His face in this world

Next, the former art director boasted about his cover photo shoot of Michael W. Smith.

> Michael's image is one of the more controlled in the entire industry. My boss was interviewing him at his ranch for the cover story and I asked if I could have 30 minutes to do an unplanned photo shoot. I literally didn't have a penny for the shoot; we had no make-up or hair teams there and I only had a few minutes after the interview.
>
> Michael came out of the interview and looked a bit puzzled as if he wasn't quite sure what we were planning to do, but he rolled with it. He had some scruff on him and a very natural look.
>
> Afterwards, I got back to the office knowing we had an amazing shot for the cover, and I put a cover concept together and sent it to management and they just freaked out. In fact, his mainstream publicist told me that hands down, that was the best photo that's ever been taken in his thirty-year career. That photo never would have happened outside the standard $15,000 photo shoot with 10 people involved and a month of production.[13]

---

13   *Ibid.*

Now you know the truth about the images you are 'allowed' to see. There are powerful and prideful creative forces at work behind the scenes, spending enormous sums of money, time and talent and using all the tricks of their trade. The sole purpose is to manipulate the images of the same artists and worship leaders who are supposed to lead us in authentic praise and worship.

No matter what compromised excuse they may give for this, it is no less than 'christianized' idol worship and the marketing of worship for a profit. This is fakery on a massive scale, masquerading as authenticity. We must firmly and clearly reject this manipulation.

Summary

Fakery is evil and a tool of the father of all lies. It is the opposite of truth, which is a non-negotiable requirement for the worshiper of God.

> Let us draw near with a true heart in full assurance of faith, having our hearts sprinkled from an evil conscience.[14]

Our aim is to worship God in truth. We cannot allow fakery to creep in unawares. How can every Christian learn to discern the difference between what is genuine and what is fake?

It starts by removing the great god Entertainment from the throne of our hearts and repenting that we ever thought its seductive fakery could help us make an acceptable offering to God. We then have to commit to a lifetime of work, to train our senses through diligent study and meditation in the Bible.

> But solid food belongs to those who are of full age, that is, those who by reason of use have their senses exercised to discern both good and evil.[15]

---

14 Hebrews 10:22.
15 Hebrews 5:14.

Let us demand that our leaders and anyone else involved in the public worship service make a commitment to keep themselves pure from fakery. Demand from them a promise that they will never use any special enhancements in our worship of God.

Chapter 14

Sheep without a shepherd

Dear Dan,

My friend, who was saved and converted out of the hard core biker scene, was with me at a church service a month ago. The worship leader started playing a Jimi Hendrix tune which my friend recognized. He became 'unglued' [upset] to hear that music in the house of God. The pastor was saved out of the Hippie Jesus revolution. He was also involved with the rock band. He said from the pulpit if you do not like the music, leave. I could hardly believe my ears when he said that. Needless to say, we did.

======================================

I wish that were the only e-mail I have received like it. But sadly I have received many more, and talked in person with many in similar dire straits: scattered not by the persecution of wicked unbelievers, but driven out of their churches by pastors who were set on modernizing their worship services by borrowing from pop culture.

These are the wounded butterflies, blown along by the storm, wings tattered and torn, left to survive on their own. They are sheep driven out of the flock by the very shepherd who was supposed to protect them. Of all the problems I have seen from the worship wars, this one hurts the most and should scandalize all who hear of it.

Some readers may think I am guilty of picking a few bad apples out of the entire orchard and that such a terrible thing is a rare and unfortunate side effect of good changes, or perhaps a simple misunderstanding. On the contrary, this is a systemic problem within the modern worship movement and it was not accidental, it was purposeful. Allow me to show you.

Driven out on purpose

For the past twenty years or more, pastors of local churches have been bombarded with church growth materials urging them to change their worship services. When a pastor decided to do so, he operated under what at first seemed to be noble motives:

- *To reach more unbelievers for Christ.* Attract them with modern worship services of relevant pop music and affirming life messages. Reduce or eliminate all the boring parts of the service. Have nothing resembling the old 'traditional' worship, because the unchurched were polled and said they didn't like that. Make the unchurched feel comfortable by removing all 'righteous' standards and dressing casually.

- *To keep the young people under age thirty from leaving the church.* They were bored too. To keep them interested, he needed to allow 'their' music in the church and even promote one of their generation to worship leader. Or create a separate alternative music service just for them.

- *To help his flock worship God more intimately.* Experience a great emotional feeling that God is really present in the worship time — just like the worship at the pastor training conferences he attended.

- *To connect his little church to the 'church at large'.* Break out of the sectarian and denominational boxes. Seek unity.

It all sounded so 'good'. But to achieve these goals and enable his church to grow, the pastor also had to deal with some unpleasant little side effects. Some of the members of his church would have legitimate concerns about the methods and outright worldliness of the entertainment-driven mindset invading their church. Others in his flock were like the ex-biker in the letter at the start of this chapter, the 'weaker brothers' of 1 Corinthians and Romans whose faith can be harmed or who can be led back into idolatry and immorality.

Rick Warren, the leader of the Purpose-Driven Church movement that has trained over 400,000 of these pastors, already had this contingency covered. Here is what he taught the pastors in 1995:

> Once you have decided on the style of music you're going to use in worship, you have set the direction of your church in far more ways than you realize. It will determine the kind of people you attract, the kind of people you keep, and the kind of people you *lose* (emphasis added).[1]

Whether he meant it that way or not, Warren's words had far-reaching consequences by emboldening other pastors to go to a place where pastors would never have gone on their own. The most popular shepherd in America declared that some sheep were expendable for the sake of the greater cause of increasing

---

1   Rick Warren, *The Purpose-Driven Church*, p.280.

church attendance numbers. He has continued this insensitive attack on good Christians with other comments such as 'the pillars of the church are just there to hold things up', a rebuke clearly targeted at members of a church who resist his programs.

Sheep in the road

Like the man traveling fast down a narrow lane in the Irish countryside, the Purpose-Driven Church (PDC) movement soon ran into sheep blocking the road. When some pastors who attended Warren's training seminar returned to their churches on fire to make bold changes, and armed with PDC books and videos to train their ministry team, they ran into stiff resistance from mature members who rightfully questioned the methods and motives.

Many pastors found themselves up against a resistance they did not expect. Some thought it was better to leave and take the 'enlightened' sheep with them to start another church. But most stayed and fought. This struggle was relayed back to the PDC leadership who recognized something had to be done to overcome the strong objections of the sheep.

Warren responded with *The Purpose-Driven Life*, a book that indoctrinated the sheep into his worship philosophies and broke down their resistance to change. Churches were offered deep discounts on the books and training videos, and tens of thousands of churches embarked upon a six-week campaign called '40 Days of Purpose'. Each sheep in the church was asked to sign a covenant to willingly participate in this.

This had the effect of isolating and culling out those sheep that were now deemed 'unfit' for the new pasture. Looking back, no one can doubt the brutal effectiveness of this strategy. I have personally seen the effect of it by talking with the sheep that did not conform.

If forty days failed to either convert or drive out the 'unfit' sheep, the pastor would continue to put on the pressure. Sermons would include statements such as these:

- 'People are dying and going to hell because you won't change your worship.'
- 'God is doing a new thing, and you need to get out of his way.'
- 'We will lose all the young people because of your personal preferences.'
- 'For those who disagree, there are other churches in this town.'

In fairness, the Purpose-Driven Church was not alone in promoting this, nor was Warren the first to say such things. The church growth movement before him freely borrowed its prime principles of operation from business management gurus. Changes devised by men of the world always leave some people behind. These business principles should be closely examined to see if they are really suitable for the church of Christ.

Off the bus

Jim Collins wrote the business best-seller *Good to Great*. He analyzed several successful businesses and decided there were four stages for building great organizations. In stage 1, the leader must 'make sure they have the right people on the bus, the wrong people off the bus, and the right people in the key seats before they figure out where to drive the bus'.[2]

The bus is a metaphor for an organization's new direction. In order to get the wrong people off the bus, Collins teaches the leader to give the person 'full opportunity to demonstrate

---

[2] Jim Collins, *Good to Great*, pp.41-64, Harper-Collins. The bus metaphor was borrowed by Collins from Ken Kesey, known for his 1960s experimentation with LSD.

that he or she might be the right person'.[3] If the person fails, the leader should act fast and be 'rigorous in the decision, but not ruthless in the implementation'.[4] In plain language, get the person off the bus quickly! That means to terminate his or her employment.

Collins deserves a lot of credit for training cold, calculating CEOs to have a little heart when firing someone. He teaches that leaders should help people 'exit with dignity and grace'.[5] But the motive he offers is not one of genuine concern for the person who is now out of work. He merely states that it is better for them to have positive feelings about the company that just fired them.

I worked on the executive management team at a software company that used *Good to Great*. We conducted a special offsite meeting where we introduced the new mission statement and objectives. When the meeting ended, as the employees filed out of the room they were told to pick up a toy bus from the table by the exit but only if they were truly 'on the bus' (e.g. in full agreement with the new program). Within a few months, several 'failed to demonstrate that he or she was the right person' and they were thrown off the bus.

What does this have to do with Christians? Through books and popular leadership seminars for pastors, business principles such as Collins' *Good to Great* are being taught for church management. Collins published a special version of *Good to Great* for non-profit organizations and it has been used by Christian ministries such as Compassion International.

Peter Drucker, the great management guru of the twentieth century, has been widely acknowledged as one of Rick Warren's mentors. Is it any wonder then that Purpose-Driven pastors now see themselves as leaders who must 'get all the right people on the bus and get all the wrong people off the bus'?

---

3   *Ibid.*
4   *Ibid.*
5   *Ibid.*

Feed my sheep

A pastor is not a CEO or VP Sales or Operations Manager. A pastor has a very special calling and job description. The word 'pastor' comes from the Latin word for 'shepherd'. The congregation of Christians in a local church is often referred to as 'the flock'.

The Old Testament is filled with references to shepherds and their sheep. This makes sense because the Jews were at first nomadic people who tended flocks and even after they settled in cities, sheep were still an important staple of their economy and diet.

The best-known reference is Psalm 23:1: 'The LORD is my shepherd; I shall not want.' God promised to 'give you shepherds according to My heart, who will feed you with knowledge and understanding'.[6] This was necessary so that 'the congregation of the LORD may not be like sheep which have no shepherd'.[7]

A pastor reports to the Chief Shepherd himself — Jesus, who called himself the good shepherd.[8] He felt compassion for the Jews, because they were distressed and downcast like sheep without a shepherd.[9]

After his resurrection and before he ascended to heaven, Jesus met with Simon Peter, the disciple of whom earlier he declared: 'I will build my church on this rock.' Jesus gave Peter the basic job description of a Christian pastor in the following scene from John chapter 21.

> So when they had eaten breakfast, Jesus said to Simon Peter, 'Simon, son of Jonah, do you love Me more than these?' He said to Him, 'Yes, Lord; You know that I love You.' He said to him, *'Feed My lambs.'*

6   Jeremiah 3:15.
7   Numbers 27:17.
8   John 10:11.
9   Matthew 9:36.

He said to him again a second time, 'Simon, son of
Jonah, do you love Me?' He said to Him, 'Yes, Lord; You
know that I love You.' He said to him, '*Tend My sheep.*'

He said to him the third time, 'Simon, son of Jonah, do
you love Me?' Peter was grieved because He said to him
the third time, 'Do you love Me?' And he said to Him, 'Lord,
You know all things; You know that I love You.' Jesus said to
him, '*Feed My sheep.*'[10]

Peter went on to become the first pastor of the first church
in Jerusalem (see Acts chapter 2) and the role model for all the
pastors to come after him. The first 'meal' for the flock was
served up by Peter in the amazing sermon he gave on the day
of Pentecost. Later, as the church grew, Peter and the other
disciples appointed deacons to care for the physical needs of
the flock so they could keep the ministry of the Word as their
main focus. In his first epistle, Peter gave instructions to pastors
which are still to be followed today.

Shepherd the flock of God which is among you, serving as
overseers, not by compulsion but willingly, not for dishonest
gain but eagerly; nor as being lords over those entrusted to
you, but being examples to the flock. And when the Chief
Shepherd appears, you will receive the crown of glory that
does not fade away.[11]

Clearly a pastor is to care for *all* the sheep entrusted to him
by the Lord. Like a good shepherd, the pastor must lead them to
green pastures to feed, a metaphor for preaching and teaching
the Word of God. He must always guard his flock from hungry
wolves (false teachers) and the roaring lion (Satan) that would
drag sheep away and destroy them.

---

10   John 21:15-17.
11   1 Peter 5:2-4.

There is one specific instance where a pastor can separate someone from the flock. We are not to keep company with any brother who is sexually immoral, covetous, an idolater, a reviler, a drunkard or an extortioner.[12] Even then the pastor and church must carefully go through a process of confrontation and pleading for repentance, before delivering this one 'to Satan for the destruction of the flesh, that his spirit may be saved in the day of the Lord Jesus.'[13]

There are other situations where we are taught by the Bible to avoid someone, but only for the purpose of shaming them so they can repent and be restored to the fellowship. We are not to associate with disorderly or unruly brethren.[14] We should also shun anyone who does not obey the doctrines of the Bible.[15] Finally, those who cause divisions and offenses that are contrary to the doctrines of the Bible should be avoided.[16]

None of these situations apply to the sheep I am writing about in this chapter. There is no room in the pastor's job description for 'getting people off the bus' simply because they cannot go along with modern worship innovations. What, then, can we say about those who have done this very thing?

> But a hireling, he who is not the shepherd, one who does not own the sheep, sees the wolf coming and leaves the sheep and flees; and the wolf catches the sheep and scatters them.[17]

Summary

It is far past time for us to put an end to this most heinous of worship war crimes. Shepherds, if you have sheep in the flock

---

12   1 Corinthians 5:11.
13   1 Corinthians 5:5.
14   2 Thessalonians 3:6.
15   2 Thessalonians 3:14.
16   Romans 16:17.
17   John 10:12.

who are conscientious objectors to modern worship innovations such as bringing in a rock band, please care for them instead of driving them off. They are not sinning against God or dividing the flock. Remember that you are the one who caused the division by introducing or simply endorsing the offense.

Every member of your flock deserves a peaceful time of public worship each week. Do not force them into violating their consciences or put them into a corner where the only choice left is leaving a church they love and need. Would it be so terrible if you chose the rescue of one sheep over indulging the modern tastes of the ninety-nine?

If you truly love Jesus — then tend to *all* his sheep entrusted to you.

Chapter 15

Where have all the hymnals gone?

The Antiques Road Show Goes to Church

Lisa, tell our viewers about what you think you have here.

I was hoping you'd tell me. I found it behind some boxes in our church's supply room.

At one of the churches where I led worship, we had nearly completed the slide into a totally contemporary style in every service and we had not used a hymnal in months. One weekend I was preparing for a Sunday service that included observance of the Lord's Supper.

There is very little contemporary music appropriate for this occasion, and even I, at this time in my worship journey, understood the need to be extra careful with music for a Communion service. I was familiar with 1 Corinthians 11, where the apostle Paul warned us not to take the Lord's Supper lightly.

So I was led back into the hymnal that I kept nearby on our piano. The Lord prompted me to select 'Near the Cross'. At first I was going to put the words on the screen, but as I practiced the song I heard the loveliest harmonies in my mind. I decided we would sing it out of the hymnal, giving people a chance to harmonize.

On Sunday morning, when it was time to prepare for Communion, I asked the congregation to open a hymnal and turn to the correct page number. There was a brief moment of confusion; I heard murmuring and shuffling. Then I said to the congregation, 'You know, the blue book stuck under the pew in front of you.' But the auditorium lights were always dimmed during our worship time, and as a result many could not find either the hymnal or the page. I asked the crew to turn up the lights.

What happened next was both sweet and sad. The light replaced the darkness and we sang out of the hymnals, with beautiful harmonies that brought tears of joy to my eyes and, from what I could see, to many other eyes in the congregation. The only accompaniment was a quiet acoustic guitar. There were no drums or electric guitars or synthesizers to smother the singing of the saints.

Many times in the past I have led hundreds in praise and worship, using both traditional and contemporary styles. But never before had I experienced such a sweet participation by everyone in the congregation. Every age group, no matter what their taste or preference, had been joined in a common song of repentance and praise to Jesus. Barriers came crashing down in this brief moment.

Then we put away the hymnals and dimmed the lights again.

I borrowed this story from my first book. Since it was published, I have heard from literally thousands of readers who said, 'You must have been in my home church, this happened here too.' Hymnals are fading from the scene, replaced by projection screens with PowerPoint slides containing the words for congregational singing.

When I first wrote about this matter, I was concerned about the potential loss of congregational singing skills that could arise as a result. In my continuing journey into worship, I have learned much more about the value of having a good hymnal in every church.[1]

Is there a problem?

Some will ask, why do we need hymnals anymore? There are Christians in large contemporary churches who have never used a hymnal, and they seem to be doing well. If needed, the words of the great hymns of the faith can be projected too. Churches with a blended service do this. Pastors and worship leaders are also quick to mention that people can sing better when their heads are not buried in a hymnal.

By cutting ties to the hymnal, a church is also free to keep up with the latest worship music innovations. All that is required is a license from Christian Copyright Licensing International (CCLI), the company that collects money from churches who use new worship songs, and then distributes that money to the copyright owner and musician.

The latest argument alleges that by eliminating hymnals we are 'going green' and doing our part to prevent global warming, because trees must be cut down to print hymnals. To some, that may seem absurd but be warned how important this factor is

---

1   For the sake of full disclosure (authenticity), let the reader be aware that I have no current financial interest in any hymnal product, so there is no agenda to sell hymnals to you!

to the under-30 Christian generation who follow those such as rock star Bono of U2, US President Obama, and certain church leaders, who are all crying out that we must save the planet.

Warnings

We also need to be aware that each seemingly 'good' reason to do away with the hymnal also brings with it some unintended consequences that should be considered before the cord is cut. For churches who have never used a hymnal, read on and you may be surprised to learn about its benefits.

Firstly, the most important element in our songs is not the music — it is the words we use. This goes right to issues of theological orthodoxy, which means conforming to established doctrine. Colossians 3:16 reminds us that psalms, hymns and spiritual songs are to be used for 'teaching and admonishing one another'. What doctrines are you learning through the lyrics of the songs at your church?

Unlike the typical American church hymnal where everyone has the words and music, our English Baptist friends use hymnals with words only. At one church I was given a gift copy of *Christian Hymns*, published by the Evangelical Movement of Wales. It contains 901 hymns. The only person in the church who has a music copy is the accompanist. The singing from these 'hymnals without music' can be more dynamic and heartfelt than singing from a PowerPoint.

After several visits to churches who use words-only hymnals, I began to realize that our singing *really is* all about the words. These congregations are taught a number of sacred hymn tunes which have been carefully vetted over many years. As they turn to a hymn, with a brief prelude the accompanist signals the hymn tune to which the words will be sung. And off they go.

Without an anchor

What happens when you do not have a hymnal? Your church is now at the whim of the worship leader to select songs with words appropriate to the doctrine of your church. This is problematic. A well-documented weakness of much modern worship music is the lyrical content, conformed more to the style of the music than anything else.

Another criticism is that the popularity of charismatic worship songs has indoctrinated non-charismatic churches into ecstatic worship through the use of much repetition of simple words in the lyrics. There are also a fair number of modern worship songs that promote an ecumenism and religious unity that would not be welcome in an independent Bible church.

A hymnal on the other hand is a faithful guardian and container of a church's doctrine. A hymnal is the product of a long and serious process undertaken by a group of musicians and theologians who are carefully chosen for their faithfulness to Christian doctrine, their knowledge of the congregations, and their sensibilities for what constitutes good sacred music as opposed to pop music. Because of the care and caution put into a good hymnal, you can trust it far more than you could ever trust any worship leader.

Slaves to fashion

Secondly, the so-called freedom to have the latest worship music can quickly become slavery to what's new for the sake of being new. When you un-tether your church from a hymnal, you are now in full reliance on the worship leader to guide the congregational music choices.

Worship leaders get their musical advice from an industry I call Worship Inc. Once they tap into any of the myriad Internet feeds for modern worship music, their hearts are drawn to the newest and the 'coolest'. Take some time and visit two websites to learn what is being pumped into your worship leader's heart and mind on a regular basis: www.ccli.com and www.worshipmusic. com. You should also remember that most worship leaders are pop/rock musicians who love secular music styles and will bring this into your church whether you agree or not.

Before you know it, the music at your church is driven by the fads and fashions of the secular music industry. The freedom of choice you thought you were getting has turned into a slavish devotion to the new and modern tastes of a wicked world.

When this occurs, the huge treasury of sacred songs passed down to us in the hymnal is largely ignored. There is a 'Modern Hymns' movement driven mainly by the same Worship Inc. machine I discussed earlier, but beware. For the most part, the musicians are simply placing the new wine of godly lyrics into the old wineskin of worldly pop music.

A hymnal, on the other hand, provides an anchor in this storm, a moderating influence to control this headlong rush into new and often offensive music styles. That should be very comforting to us.

Christianity is a religion that is arguably more about following the old paths than re-inventing worship and evangelism methods for every generation. Consider:

- We serve the Ancient of Days, not the god of what's happening now.
- Our guidebook for faith and worship was completed in the first century A.D., and 2,000 years later we are still striving faithfully to maintain the 'old words' as closely as possible.
- We are still to avoid idolatry in any form, based on the 4,000-year-old example of an ancient desert tribe.
- Conversion to the faith is still accomplished by God using the old-fashioned way.

I could go on and on about the divinely ordained backwardness and narrowness of our faith and the benefits inherent in this. Jesus said, 'Enter by the narrow gate; for wide is the gate and broad is the way that leads to destruction, and there are many who go in by it. Because narrow is the gate and difficult is the way which leads to life, and there are few who find it.'[2]

A music minister who has the hymnal at his disposal will be influenced to choose music first from a reliable and trusted source, and then look more carefully for new songs.[3] I argue this will preserve far more diversity in our Christian praise, by encouraging a balance of songs from across many centuries of Christian experience.

Screen test

Thirdly, the proponents of replacing hymnals with words on a screen assured us people would praise God in song much better since they would be looking up rather than having their heads buried in the hymnal. After twenty-five years of the experiment, can we stop and examine the reality?[4]

My readers have sent me countless examples of how the singing at their churches declined after the transition to the screen. More people are standing around watching and listening to the performers. Lest you accuse them of being biased towards the hymnal, what I found most fascinating was how many readers said they were fully in favor of the change at first!

When the arguments in favor of replacing the hymnals with PowerPoint were first proposed, I think the musicians knew

---

2   Matthew 7:13-14.
3   I take the position that there are some good hymns being written today. Before choosing a new hymn for public worship, first I encourage that each church should have a carefully written musical guideline to inform this choice, one that is biblically based, respectful of good traditions and anchored by a good hymnal.
4   Contrary to rumors, I have never called for a complete ban of projecting lyrics on a screen. I see some value in its rare use for introducing a new hymn to the congregation, or supplementing a hymnal since no one hymnal contains every useful hymn.

better but most kept silent. The use of hand-held hymnals does not in and of itself prevent anyone from singing better. On the contrary: some evidence points in the opposite direction. If hand-held music were such a problem, every choir would have ditched their music eons ago.

But the leaders of this movement had no interest in the advice of 'traditional' church musicians. As a former song-leader who was later repositioned as a worship leader, and with many experiences leading congregational singing, I saw a different agenda at work behind the removal of hymnals.

Contemporary church growth leaders have been very open to proclaim that church music had to change in order to grow the church. Sacred music was passé, to be replaced as quickly as possible by pop/rock music because that's what the unchurched listen to on their car radios.

The hymnals occupied a precarious position in the churches, similar to the elder members of a church who have been called 'pillars of the church who only hold things up' — meaning, of course, that they stand in the way of change. To change the music of a church to the degree sought by these leaders meant the hymnals must go; or as you saw in the story at the beginning of this chapter, simply let them collect dust.

Modern-day Pharisees

Some in the modern worship movement also have shown a 'holier than thou' attitude about how people should physically praise and worship God. As a former worship leader, I experienced first-hand how the leaders thought the authentic worshipers were those who looked up during singing, smiled angelically to show they were with us, and then closed their eyes and raised their hands during the song. How, we thought, can one truly worship God this way while inconveniently holding onto a heavy hymn-book?

We were so blind we failed to realize that we were focusing on the externals of worship more than what is in the heart! How ironic that this was a worship movement built on the credo of 'While man looks on the outward appearance, God looks at the heart; so don't judge us for how we worship.' Here we were judging external worship, just like the traditional hypocrites we criticized.

Summary

A hymnal is very different from the contemporary 'worship song of the month'. There is the benefit of relying on the wisdom of godly men and women who very carefully assembled the hymnal. No hymnal is perfect, of course, but we can trust the vast majority of selections without the need to examine each song and composer.

The pastor who claims that he will rigorously examine every modern worship song before allowing its use in his church takes on a terrible burden that will detract from his time preparing messages, discipling the flock, and doing the work of an evangelist. I think that pastor means well, but in practice he delegates this to a worship leader who is less qualified to defend the faith and the flock.

When we throw out the hymnals, we also throw out God-given protections against doctrinal drift, heresy and shocking musical worldliness. We turn over the musical catechism of our children to an ecumenical music industry driven by the worst fashions and lusts of this present age.

It is past time to end the experiment and invest again in a good hymnal. Buy one for every home too. To anyone in a contemporary church who complains about the cost, ask them how much they spend on their worship/multimedia technology budget. The cost of hymnals may pale in comparison.

Chapter 16

Heaven can wait

During the apostle John's remarkable vision on the island of Patmos, God revealed to him that there will be music in heaven. One of the most breathtaking passages in all Scripture records an amazing song of praise in the throne room of God. The 'four living creatures and the twenty-four elders ... sang a new song.'[1]

But what kind of music is it? Is it music as we know it, with staves and scales, chords and canons? Will there be melody, harmony and rhythm as we know them here?[2]

We can only imagine

We have no idea. We are not given any details about the music, perhaps to enable us to concentrate on the words. It will certainly be 'a new song', but as a British preacher has said, 'No composer can estimate its value, no instrument can play its harmony, no

1   Revelation 5:8-9.
2   *Can We Rock the Gospel?* p.231.

voice can pronounce its beauty, no modulator can convey its height or its depth; this song is arranged to please the ear of God.'[3]

Truly, we can 'only imagine', to quote the famous song, and therefore must be careful not to read into heavenly worship what we do on earth. But this inconvenience has not stopped many worship leaders and pastors from declaring that our earthly worship should emulate the throne-room scene that begins in Revelation chapter 4.

In rapturous language these leaders describe the awesome scene, bringing chills to the listener, urging everyone to worship more like the elders in the throne room. Worship seminars, sermons, books and modern worship albums have been devoted to this subject.

We are told that we will be worshiping for all eternity like this, so shouldn't we start here on earth to prepare for it? The people who teach this also use the 'draw near' passages in Hebrews to reinforce what they see as a mandate for all worshipers on earth to imitate the throne-room scene. They also tell us a great cloud of witnesses is watching us from heaven, cheering on our worship here on earth.[4]

Wrong turn

Warning: this could be another wrong turn on the journey into worship. Rather than inspiring a great sense of awe and reverence for our earthly worship, the emulation of throne-room worship has led to just the opposite for some Christians. Not only is it a pursuit of the unattainable, we are also subjected to all manner of silly 'imaginations' of what it will be like when we are worshiping in heaven.

---

3   William Freel, *Survival? God's Fabulous Future*, The Berrico Group of Companies, 1976.
4   Hebrews 12:1. The cloud of witnesses are not there to cheer for our worship. They represent the faithful from chapter 11 and are there as examples to encourage us so we will not abandon the faith.

After an especially emotional music performance or congregational song, some leaders love to proclaim: 'This is just a preview of what it will be like in heaven!' Others exclaim: 'If the music in your version of heaven isn't this good, then I don't want to spend eternity with you!' Stop and consider for a minute: how *low* have these people set the bar for heaven's music?

Some say all music styles will be represented in heaven and to each his own. Others claim that heaven will be a big rock music concert. The leader of a ladies' group at a Southern Baptist church showed a video that pictured heaven as a massive rock party, after which she then played some loud and chaotic rock music to show them how wonderful heaven will be.

When one lady disagreed with her, the leader replied, 'You have your opinion and I have mine. Do you really think that we would just be angels with wings, flying all around, strumming on harps all the time?' 'No,' the objector answered, 'I only believe what the Bible says about heaven.'

Turning to leave, the leader retorted, 'Well, if you don't like it, then don't watch it!'[5]

This is hardly a biblical response. But that is the type of silly response that accompanies circular reasoning about worship. Follow the logic:

1. They love to use rock music (or insert their favorite music style) for worship on earth.
2. There is music in the throne room of heaven.
3. Therefore, it *must* be their music!

This is symptomatic of the problems we encounter when attempting to project the heavenly throne-room scene into our earthly sanctuaries, or vice versa. Wish as we might, we cannot come close to worshiping like that, nor should we waste our time trying.

---

5   *Can We Rock the Gospel?* p.26.

Bursting the balloon

I find several reasons to burst this brightly-colored balloon.

1. Any attempts we make here on earth would come so pitifully short of what God requires in heaven, as to insult him for even trying to mimic the throne room on earth. When it comes to what constitutes heavenly sounding music, Christians don't seem to agree on much and we are left to argue which is more heavenly sounding. This is one area where personal preferences will continue to reign on this side of heaven.
2. Well meaning and inspirational though it starts, this degenerates into another attempt to create an emotional and ecstatic experience on earth. In the end, this will require more fakery and gimmicks to sustain such feelings.
3. The Lord Jesus and the Apostles never asked us to worship like heaven. The apostle John had every opportunity as he gave instructions from Jesus to the churches in Revelation. Where was the instruction to 'worship like the throne room'? As mentioned in earlier chapters, the *proskuneo* worship found in the throne room disappeared after Jesus left the earth.

Directions from heaven

We can, however, draw important principles from the throne-room scene, which can help us regulate our worship here on earth.

1. Our prayers are the only earthly things that count in the heavenly worship. In the throne-room scene in the book of Revelation, the elders offer golden bowls full of incense 'which are the prayers of the saints'.[6] There is a very detailed picture

---

6   Revelation 5:8.

of this. 'Then another angel, having a golden censer, came and stood at the altar. He was given much incense, that he should offer it with the prayers of all the saints upon the golden altar which was before the throne. And the smoke of the incense, with the prayers of the saints, ascended before God from the angel's hand.'[7]

As part of God's instructions to Moses on how to worship him through the earthly tabernacle, there was to be a golden altar of incense in the tent of meeting placed directly in front of the veil that covered the Holy of Holies. The incense was to burn continually.[8]

While Zechariah, the father of John the Baptist, attended to the altar of incense in the temple performing his priestly duties, 'The whole multitude of the people was praying outside at the hour of incense',[9] as was the custom of the Jews. Once a year on the Day of Atonement, the High Priest took a golden bowl of incense into the Holy of Holies and offered it before the presence of God.

After Christ's once-for-all atonement for sin and the abolishment of the old worship practices, the incense of the earthly temple is no longer needed. The incense in this passage is illustrative of Christ's merits, the only basis on which God hears and accepts our prayers. Through the merits of Christ, when we pray in his name the Holy Spirit translates our frail human words of prayer and supplication into an acceptable offering in the heavenly sanctuary before God.[10]

2. May Jesus Christ be praised — with very specific words! In the throne-room scenes we find the lyrical model for Christian praise songs, and for the spoken praise and prayer each of us offers as the sacrifice of praise.

---

7   Revelation 8:3-4.
8   Exodus chapter 30.
9   Luke 1:10.
10   Romans 8:26.

In Revelation chapter 5 we see Jesus pictured in two amazing ways: first, as the Lion of Judah; and second, as the Lamb that was slain. Jesus receives worship from the elders similar to God the Father. The elders fall down before Jesus, then they sing a new song to him: 'Thou art worthy to take the book, and to open the seals thereof: for thou wast slain, and hast redeemed us to God by thy blood out of every kindred, and tongue, and people, and nation.'[11]

Next everyone in the throne room — the living creatures, the elders and ten thousands upon ten thousands of angels — say[12] with a loud voice: 'Worthy is the Lamb who was slain to receive power and riches and wisdom, and strength and honor and glory and blessing!'[13]

Finally, every created thing which is in heaven and on the earth and under the earth and on the sea, and all things in them, are heard saying, 'Blessing and honor and glory and power be to Him who sits on the throne, and to the Lamb, for ever and ever!'[14]

The apostle Paul gave us a similar model for praising Christ in Philippians 2:9-11.

3. *Amen is the applause of heaven, and a proper response when we worship God and Christ.*

- 'Then the four living creatures said, "Amen!"'[15]
- 'All the angels stood around the throne and the elders and the four living creatures, and fell on their faces before the throne and worshiped God, saying: "Amen! Blessing and glory and wisdom, thanksgiving and honor and power and might, be to our God for ever and ever. Amen."'[16]

---

11 Revelation 5:9 (AV).
12 Note they do not sing, they speak; the Greek word is *lego*.
13 Revelation 5:12.
14 Revelation 5:13.
15 Revelation 5:14.
16 Revelation 7:11-12.

- 'And the twenty-four elders and the four living creatures fell down and worshiped God who sat on the throne, saying, "Amen! Alleluia!"'[17]

We clap to show applause for men and women here on earth. But shouldn't we treat God's worship differently and mimic the heavenly Amen?

4. God is awesome and holy, and anyone who claims to worship him must never forget this. The throne-room scenes portray a God so mighty and fearsome that for eternity there is always one group after another falling flat on their faces in humble worship. All of our worship offerings must be bathed in this never-changing view of God. Thanks be to God that Jesus is 'covering' for us before the throne, and to the Holy Spirit who translates our prayers into an acceptable offering in heaven.

Summary

While we can learn important principles from throne-room worship that can inform our worship practices, attempts to emulate the awe and rapture of heaven here on earth will always fall pitiably short of the mark. Worse, they can lead us into vain imaginations about the music in heaven and wasting time on things that do not matter at all to God.

We have plenty enough direction on how to worship God to keep us busy while we're still here on earth. We do not need to imagine.

---

[17] Revelation 19:4.

Chapter 17

Yes, David danced;
but you're not David

Dear Dan,

Could you help me with something that happened at my church last night? We sang a song entitled 'Undignified'. It was about how undignified we were going to be in our worship. It bothered me. The chorus was 'Na, na, na, na, na, na — Hey!' On the word 'hey', many pumped their fists in the air. Some spontaneously broke into dance.

Later, I e-mailed my pastor asking how we could worship a holy God that way, and he sent me to 2 Samuel 6:12-22. He said Michal judged David's worship but David said he would become even more undignified than this.

I am confused, even saddened, by this. Am I just judging others?

Diane

Dear Diane,

You are right to be concerned about what happened at your church and the wrong use of this Bible story in an attempt to justify it. I am familiar with the song and the phrase 'undignified worship'. The lyrics say:

> I will dance, I will sing, to be mad for my king,
> Nothing Lord is hindering the passion in my soul,
> Some would say it's foolishness, but
> I'll become even more undignified than this.[1]

Where did 'undignified worship' originate? Once upon a time, some young rock 'n' roll worship leaders were criticized by other Christians for 'undignified' behavior in public worship. It is very important to now remind the reader exactly what type of behavior was under fire.

These young worship leaders were playing loud rock music and imitating the physical actions one would normally associate with a secular rock concert. They incited the 'worshipers' to act just like the crowd at a rock concert — wild, animalistic body movements, fist-pumping, body surfing and other actions not usually found in a church service.

Rather than pausing to consider if their actions were offensive to others, or perhaps simply the result of youthful indiscretion, the young rockers searched the Bible to justify their behavior. In an astounding feat of circular reasoning, they found the story of David dancing before the ark (2 Samuel 6:15 and 1 Chronicles 15:29), and adopted it as their battle cry against the traditionalists.

Today it is still a favorite argument offered in defense of the modern worship movement with its 'undignified' pop music and dance. I hear this defense almost as much as 'the church borrowed tunes from bars' or 'music is amoral'. As the latter two excuses are fast fading into oblivion, now is a good time to relegate this one to the dustbin of silly excuses for inappropriate worship.

---

1   Words and Music by Matt Redman, © ThankYou Music.

Facts are stubborn things

Was Michal judging David's worship style? Can modern worship leaders use this passage to justify their desire to act as undignified as they please, without restraint? What were David and Michal actually doing here?

Let's examine the story. David was leading a Jewish ceremonial parade to return the Ark of the Covenant to Jerusalem. It was an exciting and sober event: exciting, because the Ark was returning from Philistine captivity to Jerusalem; sober, because a priest had died earlier at the hand of God for improperly touching the Ark.

Instead of wearing his usual royal robes, David was dressed in a white linen ephod and robe, priestly garments symbolizing righteousness. He was not 'prancing about' in his undergarments, as some have wrongly implied! The ephod was a sacred tunic worn by the priests during their worship to God, and sometimes worn by others.[2] Fine white linen is a symbol of the righteousness and purity of the saints.[3] Matthew Henry commented that 'righteousness is the best ornament of a minister. Holiness towards God ... [is a] habit for ministers the necessity of which there is no dispute.'[4]

David's dancing was in the Jewish male tradition of leaping and whirling, springing about joyfully, and skipping along with glee. For a Jewish man to show his delight in the Lord in this manner apparently was acceptable behavior to the onlookers.

There is no record of criticism from the onlookers during the parade. The Levites, known for their fierce defense of holy behavior in all things related to worship, did not rebuke David. Only one person objected — his wife Michal, daughter of the former King Saul. From her window overlooking the parade

---

2   1 Samuel 2:18.
3   Revelation 19:8.
4   *Matthew Henry Commentary* on Psalm 132:8.

route, she saw David whirling and leaping and despised him in her heart.

Was she judging David's style of worship? No! She was judging his behavior as unbecoming for a great soldier and monarch leading a procession in front of his nation. As queen of Israel, Michal was no doubt concerned about the royal family's image. Her reaction had nothing to do with how David worshiped the Lord. She thought David had acted like one of the 'base fellows' (commoners), not as a king of Israel.

Michal had problems of her own. Raised as a king's daughter, her motive for criticizing David was probably related to her opinion of how a king should properly act in front of servants. In those days, her treatment of David was also an act of extreme disrespect from a wife to a husband. This was a truly dysfunctional marriage.

David's response was devastating. He reminded her that God chose him to be king, not anyone from Saul's household. That would have hurt her deeply. To make his point clear, David said if she thought that was undignified, he would become even *more* undignified than this.

You're not David

These are the facts. Michal was not judging a worship or music style. David's dancing and dress were not 'undignified'; both were within the bounds of Jewish practice. He was most certainly not trying to shock the crowd with Philistine dance moves or edgy Hittite music. And David did not actually follow through with his threat to Michal to become 'more undignified'. He was simply making a point.

Isn't it therefore foolish for anyone today to claim these verses as support for unrelated 'undignified' behavior during public worship? To compare a modern-day Christian's wild gyrations copied direct from his or her experience with ungodly music to David's dancing and praise, and then use David to claim a refuge from any and all legitimate criticism of their 'bad' behavior, seems to me either the height of arrogance or the depth of ignorance. Worse than that, comparing sincerely concerned Christian brethren to Michal reeks of the same ill-judged, disrespectful attitude shown by some modern worshipers.

I call on worship leaders and the preachers who support them to stop using this passage in an attempt to cover today's bad behavior. Further, they will need to pro-actively correct their followers who slavishly repeat this myth as if it were truth.

Lessons learned

Now that we have debunked the 'Undignified' myth, let's focus on the authentic lessons we can draw from this story.

1. *David had great respect for God's worship traditions.* He played by the rules. We should not be so quick, as some are today, to 'despise' Christian worship traditions that are based on the same respect for reverence and propriety in public worship as David showed.
2. *David removed his royal robes — a symbol of his earthly power and position.* He put on the linen ephod — a symbol of purity in worship. Likewise, we should remove our worldly affections, clothe ourselves with the righteousness of Christ, and be holy when we praise and worship God.
3. *David humbled himself before the Lord —* He said, 'I will be humble in my own sight.'[5] We too should humble ourselves before the Lord when we draw near to worship.[6]

---

5   2 Samuel 6:22.
6   James 4:6-10.

4. *Michal judged David on appearances.* She was more concerned about the royal image than the inner man. We too must be careful not to judge others based only on externals.

Summary

Diane, after considering the evidence, it is my firm belief that the story of David and Michal cannot be used to justify what just happened in your church service.

A brother in the Lord Jesus Christ, for his glory and honor,

Dan

Colossians 3:16

Part III

U-turn

C. S. Lewis once commented that when a person is headed in the wrong direction, sometimes the best way to make progress is to turn around, go backwards and get on the right road.[1]

---

1   C. S. Lewis, *Mere Christianity*, p.36.

Chapter 18

U-turns and course corrections

'Re-routing ... go to the next crossroad and make a U-turn.' That is what my GPS tells me whenever I miss a turn and drive off in the wrong direction. Sometimes that is accidental but there are other times when I decide to take my *own* route to the destination. I may think I know the best route — which in my mind is always the fastest and easiest way. Perhaps a friend told me about a short-cut that everyone else is taking. After all, a GPS can be wrong sometimes.

Many sincere Christians have traveled far down the road of modern worship on our own route; but I believe we 'sincerely' went off in the wrong direction. It is time to stop and turn around. A GPS may sometimes be wrong, but *God's Positioning System* (the Word of God) is always true and will faithfully keep us on the right road.

Re-routing

What road are you on? Does your worship tend to be 'all about the music', crowding out the other vital acts of worship? Is your worship eerily similar to the pop entertainment methods of the world? Have you spent your time, passion and money on worship practices that may seem emotionally fulfilling and exciting, but miss the mark of what God has asked us to do for him?

If you want to make a U-turn and return to the old paths, first you may need to unload some extra baggage that could slow you down or tempt you to return to the wrong roads. Here are some personal reformations to consider.

Extinguish your strange fire

'Then Nadab and Abihu, the sons of Aaron, each took his censer and put fire in it, and put incense on it, and offered profane fire before the LORD, which he had not commanded them. So fire went out from the LORD and devoured them, and they died before the LORD. And Moses said to Aaron, "This is what the LORD spoke, saying: 'By those who come near Me I must be regarded as holy; and before all the people I must be glorified.'"'[2]

This is a tragic story about sudden death at the first tabernacle worship service, and a lesson for all future worshipers of God. What is the meaning of 'profane' (AV — strange) fire and how can it warn us today about our own worship practices?

Nadab and Abihu were priests set apart to offer daily worship to God. This included an offering of incense to be burnt on top of their fire pans (AV — censer). In Exodus chapter 30, God spoke to Moses and commanded him to build the altar of incense for the tabernacle. God also gave very specific instructions on the incense and how the priests were to present it when they came near to God.

- This incense must be offered twice a day (morning and twilight) as a perpetual offering.[3]

---

2   Leviticus 10:1-3.
3   Exodus 30:7-8.

- Do not offer 'strange' incense.[4] The Hebrew meaning of strange is 'something foreign or profane'. It is connected to adultery — which is often used by God to describe the sin of idolatry whenever Israel adopted the worship practices of the nations around them.
- Offer only the sacred incense.[5] God told them to make a special concoction of incense using a special recipe. He warned them not to use the same incense or recipe to make perfume for their own use. This was to be holy, sacred incense. Anyone who disobeyed was to be cut off from his people (in other words, shunned).

Nadab and Abihu knew all about 'strange' incense and were well aware of God's command never to use anything profane in their worship. But what was 'strange' about the fire they brought in their fire pans? After all, weren't the priests instructed in Leviticus to put fire on the bronze altar and arrange wood on the fire?[6] And the priests were told a few chapters later that the fire on the altar must never be allowed to go out.[7] So far, it seems that the priests were to light the fire.

Not so fast. In Leviticus chapter 9, after being consecrated and purified, the priests of Israel begin the first worship service of the tabernacle. God told them to sacrifice animals on the bronze altar for the sins of the people. And before any priest could light a fire on the altar, God himself provided the fire!

And fire came out from before the LORD and consumed the burnt offering and the fat on the altar.[8]

The fire came down from heaven and was to be carefully preserved. It was unlawful to use any other fire in the service of

---

4   Exodus 30:9.
5   Exodus 30:37-38.
6   Leviticus 1:7.
7   Leviticus 6:13.
8   Leviticus 9:24.

God. All other fire was forbidden.[9]

Nadab and Abihu did not use the approved sacred fire that came from God. They disobeyed a direct command, made their own fires and used coals kindled by their own hands to burn the sacred incense in the presence of God. The penalty for this disobedient worship was instant death.

Such was the holiness of God, that he made an example of these disobedient and willful worshipers so that, for ever after, all who would worship God are warned that 'by those who come near Me I must be regarded as holy.'[10]

Hundreds of years later in Israel, the holy fire from the Lord had long gone out and the priests were thoroughly corrupted, offering profane offerings on the altar. God told them not to 'kindle fire on My altar in vain'. He said, 'I have no pleasure in you, nor will I accept an offering from your hands.'[11]

What is the application for Christians today? Some preachers and authors have condemned rock music as 'strange fire', using this passage to warn Christians of the dire consequences that could befall them when that music style is mixed with worship. While I am certainly no fan of rock music in God's service,[12] that application seems too simplistic. And we have not yet witnessed the fire of God consuming a worship leader offering rock.

I think this passage is there to warn us not to take God's Name in vain nor to approach him with any and all 'profane' things. We must be very careful not to do anything to dishonor God's Holy Name by mixing our own profane concoctions with it. We should not employ anything that is related to the evil and idolatrous practices of our surrounding culture, because to do so would obviously dishonor the Holy Name.

To the clever worship leader who retorts that 'It's only what is in my heart that counts', the story of Nadab and Abihu should

---

9   Matthew Poole's *Commentary on Leviticus*; Adam Clarke's *Commentary on Leviticus*.
10   Leviticus 10:3.
11   Malachi 1:10.
12   See my books concerning the problems of employing rock and other pop music styles for worship and evangelism. *Why I Left the Contemporary Christian Music Movement* (2002) and *Can We Rock the Gospel?* (2006). Available from EP Books.

silence him or her. It demonstrates that preserving the holy honor of God in front of his people matters as much as what one claims is hidden inside one's heart.

If we fail to honor God's Name in our worship, he may not kill us immediately with fire. But there are still consequences in this life. How could we expect God to answer our prayers and praise if we offer them up on a strange and profane fire we kindled from our own sinful flesh using wood, hay and stubble from a wicked culture? How can anyone expect blessings if they treat God's Holy Name with such contempt? Even more serious and fearful to consider is whether a person who worships God in such an unholy manner is even a true child of God.

Demolish your high places

Ancient Israel was surrounded by tribes who worshiped false gods. The false worshipers performed their rituals on the high places — enclosures on the top of mountains or little hills, consecrated for practicing the rites of idolatry. They were usually placed on a very high spot to enable the worshipers to have a better view of the rising sun, which was worshiped as a god.[13]

Before the Exodus, some of God's people worshiped him on high places. But after God gave his Law to Israel, high places were forbidden and whenever set up, they were ordered to be destroyed. As Israel prepared to enter the land of Canaan, God told Moses to instruct the leaders to drive out the inhabitants of the land, destroy their idols and 'demolish all their high places'.[14]

But God's people did not always obey. They continually sinned by mixing the worship of God with idol worship practices. This is called syncretism, the combination of different forms of belief or practice into one religion. The altitude of the place itself was not a problem; Abraham worshiped God on Mount Moriah, a

---

13 Jamieson-Fausset-Brown *Commentary* on Lev. 26:30.
14 Numbers 33:52.

high place. The problem was disobedience! God did not want his people mixed up in any form of pagan worship practice or practicing their religion in a way that resembled idol worship.

Today's 'high places' are more about method and style than about physical locations. We live in a world that uses entertainment to worship and serves the spirit-gods of this world, which are the lust of the flesh, the lust of the coveting eye, and the boastful pride of life.[15] A. W. Tozer reminded us how deeply the great god of Entertainment has infected the worship of the church.

> Isn't there a difference between worship and entertainment? The church that can't worship must be entertained. And men who can't lead a church to worship must provide the entertainment. That is why we have the great evangelical heresy here today — the heresy of religious entertainment...[16]
>
> Millions of evangelicals throughout the world have devoted themselves to religious entertainment. They don't know that it's as much heresy as the counting of beads or splashing of holy water. We cannot deny that this attitude is found in much of current Christianity...[17]
>
> It is not hard to see why the great god Entertainment is so ardently worshiped by so many. For there are millions who cannot live without amusement; life without some form of entertainment for them is simply intolerable...[18]
>
> So today we have the astonishing spectacle of millions of dollars being poured into the unholy job of providing earthly entertainment for the so-called sons of heaven. Many churches have become poor theatres where producers peddle their shoddy wares with the full approval

---

15   1 John 2:16.
16   Tozer on *Worship and Entertainment*, p.115.
17   *Ibid.* p.114.
18   *Ibid.* p.100.

of evangelical leaders who can even quote a holy text in defense of their delinquency. And hardly a man dares to raise his voice against it.[19]

Does your worship include popular entertainment methods lifted directly from the high places of a wicked culture? Do you attend a church where the leaders seem more interested in creating a first-class show and spend enormous sums of money to imitate Hollywood and Nashville production values? Is there a drum set sitting on a high place in your sanctuary?

If you answered 'yes' to one or more of these questions, it may be time to demolish the high places in your heart. And then remove some of the physical ones in your church.

Throw out the dove sellers

'So [Jesus] made a whip out of cords, and drove all from the temple area, both sheep and cattle; he scattered the coins of the money-changers and overturned their tables. To those who sold doves he said, "Get these out of here! How dare you turn my Father's house into a market!"'[20]

The Lord Jesus was very angry at people who were profiting from the worship of God by turning the Father's house into a marketplace. This is also a sober warning for those involved in today's marketing-driven industry I call 'Worship Inc.'

Driven mainly by musical performers and those who promote them, Worship Inc. is a multi-million dollar industry pouring profits into the coffers of secular companies such as EMI Group or CBS. As with any other entertainment enterprise, Worship Inc. relies on marketing gimmicks to stimulate demand for new products.

---

19   *Ibid.* p.112.
20   John 2:15-16 (NIV).

They are today's dove sellers who turn the Father's house into a marketplace. God's Spirit dwells in each believer; we are the Father's house now. According to Jesus, any marketing of worship for profit is wrong and must be removed.

You may be one of the many Christians who became 'hooked on' new worship music. You follow worship artists no differently than you followed (or still follow) secular musicians. You are a fan (short for 'fanatic'), you post comments on their web pages, and you join the inner circle on their websites so you can have first notice of concerts or new song releases. When a new CD comes out, you are the first to download the new tracks to your iPod. You are passionate about the music and the artists, sharing your love for them with friends on the Internet.

But this is not what the worship of God is to be about. This is no more than sanctified 'idol-worship' of Christian stars. And you are a willing victim of one of the most disingenuous marketing machines ever devised. Think of it: the same people who persuaded Christians that the best way to worship God is through new worship songs have also created a powerful motivation to keep you buying their new music.

Be radical and resist this corruption of worship. Follow Jesus, not the worship-music stars marketed by a corrupt industry. Lest you think I am too harsh on them, read Steve Camp's 107 Theses, a call for reformation in the CCM industry.[21] Then consider this more recent confession from an industry insider:

> How do you keep the worship pure while having to answer to business people and a marketing team? ... What is more important ... kingdom impact or units sold? Can you have both? This caused me to begin to ponder everything about our modern idea of worship.[22]

---

21   stevenjcamp.blogspot.com/2006/10/still-pounding-on-wittenbergs-doora.html
22   Alisa Childers, formerly with the CCM band ZOEgirl. alisachilders.blogspot.com/2009/07/my-journey-into-worship.html

Let's be fair and apply the same resistance to any form of Christian music idolatry, no matter the genre — pop, classical, Celtic etc. Let us each clean out our own temple: 'Do you not know that you are the temple of God?'[23] It's time to throw out those who sell doves.

Return to reverence and respect

Can your worship be described as 'reverent'? Earlier in the book we looked at the importance of reverence (literally, a healthy fear of God) as fundamental to pleasing God in our acts of worship. Remember Hebrews 12:28-29, where we learned that our acts of worship to God should be offered in a continual attitude of reverence and awe because he is still the same consuming fire that destroyed Nadab and Abihu.

What does 'reverent worship' look like? Reverent worshipers are more concerned about the holiness of God's Name than the relevance of the methods they use. Reverent worshipers do not mix the praise of holy God with vulgar musical styles borrowed from the most unholy sources. Reverent worshipers would rather be anywhere than the typical worship service full of banalities, jokes and entertainment tricks. Reverent worshipers do not address God as their best buddy.

Next to reverent worship is worship that respects elder Christians who practice ancient traditions. One of the glaring failures of the modern worship movement is how it split the church into age groups based on musical preferences, and emphasized that youth must be served over wisdom. Elders who complained that the worship service became too worldly were mocked and marginalized by pastors who seem determined to cater to what the apostle Paul called 'youthful lusts'.[24]

---

23   1 Corinthians 3:16.
24   2 Timothy 2:22.

I believe this tendency to create a 'youth church' or 'youth-oriented worship service' is unnatural and unhealthy. The Christian church is a family and the members of a family ought to demonstrate their common solidarity, rather than their differences. The wisdom of elders is to be respected over youthful passions.

Summary

What road have you been traveling on? If you found yourself heading down the wrong road, then it's time to stop and turn around — or to use biblical language, to repent. To start back on the right road, first you may have to extinguish your strange fire, break down the high places you've worshiped on, throw the dove sellers out of your temple, and return to reverence for God and respect for elders.

The destination is worth the reformation.

Part IV

On the road again

Chapter 19

On the road again

We have traveled a long way to get back on the road of a journey into worship that pleases God. Here is a quick review of the ground we have covered.

First, we confronted the popular myth that worship is all about the music. We realized that sometimes our devotion to music, new or old, keeps us from the other things we should be doing to worship God.

Next, we learned how to worship God in the way that he accepts and expects, with an emphasis on discovering the basics of worship from the Word of God. For most, this was an introduction to the sacrifices of the New Testament worshiper: the sacrifice of our bodies, the sacrifice of praise and the sacrifice of *koinonia*.

We then looked at the differences and similarities of private and public worship. We examined the essential components of Christian worship services taught in the Bible and reliable church traditions. We found some components that are overlooked or ignored at some churches, and challenged ourselves to restore balance.

Next we spent time looking into the wrong turns and cul-de-sacs of the modern worship movement. We examined the worship leader movement and challenged churches to reconsider this because of the unintended consequences. The problem of using fakery to stimulate intense feelings of worship was exposed.

We looked into the consequence of abandoning the use of hymnals and challenged the 'David danced' myth. Finally we considered the need for a U-turn to get back on the road, and looked at areas where we may need to repent before we can get started on the way back.

For those who have come this far, I am deeply grateful and give glory to our God. You are now on a road that is thinly traveled these days. Many other Christians remain in heavy traffic on the freeway of a culturally relevant worship driven by emotions and popularity with the world.

To many, it looks like the right road simply because that is where the popular people are. Do not let that discourage you. Stay now on the straight and narrow road,[1] on the old paths where the good way of the Lord is found.[2]

Freedom to worship

When you are on this road, there is a new freedom to worship God as he intended. This is not about the First Amendment of the United States Constitution, where freedom to worship was enshrined in the laws of the land. This is about freedom from the false expectations to worship God in a certain way that is dictated by the commandments of men.

This is about freedom from conforming our worship to the fashions and fads of the corrupt spirit of this age we live in. On

---

1   Matthew 7:13-20.
2   Jeremiah 6:16.

this road, we are more concerned about the holiness of God than about popularity or image. We can now ignore without regret or anxiety the voices of change and modernity that are always pushing the 'new way to worship God'.

This is about freedom from the 'me-monster', the 'just God and me' worship mentality advocated by some popular Christian preachers and authors. Christian 'me-monsters' think they can worship God in any way that suits them the best. They were created, nurtured and discipled by books peddling narcissistic notions such as this:

> Many Christians seem stuck in a worship rut ... because they force themselves to use devotional methods that don't fit the way God uniquely shaped them. God wants you to be yourself. The best style of worship is the one that most authentically represents your love for God, based on the background and personality God gave you.[3]

When did individual Christians get the right to choose the style of worship that fits them individually? This may come across to some as good self-help advice for misfits, but it is certainly not biblical worship advice and it is completely foreign to reliable and proven worship traditions. This advice may inevitably lead to:

- *Self-delusion*: I am the judge of what's right for my own worship;
- *Perpetual church splits*: today I feel like worshiping with other people just like me;
- and in due course to *a sad and thoroughly unchristian individualism*: no one else understands my personal worship needs so I'll stay home and design my own experience on the Internet.

---

3   Rick Warren, *The Purpose-Driven Life*, p.102.

Oddly enough, what would seem like the ultimate freedom to worship individually as one pleases is actually *not* freedom at all. It leads to bondage to the god of this world and to those individual passions that he wants to keep us enslaved to.

This is the same evil one who told Eve in the Garden of Eden that she could be like God, knowing everything and therefore free to make her own decisions and take control of her own life. When I speak of freedom, I speak instead of the freedom from fear and anxiety that we can have only when we are firmly planted in God's will.

Freedom from artificial stimulants

There is another valuable freedom to be gained by taking the narrow road. Now that we know music is not the main means of worship, we are free from our dependence on artificial stimulation to produce those 'spiritual' feelings at each worship service or in our private devotions.

No longer is the quality of our worship experience dependent on the clever programing of a musical package intended to bring us up and let us down emotionally. The worship leader or song leader can cajole us all he or she wants about not looking like we are worshiping and needing to raise our hands or fall to the ground or jump up and down, and we can cheerfully ignore him without any eternal consequence.

We are also free to ignore the use of mood lighting to create a sense of reverence or joy, or video screen stimulation with beautiful shots of nature to invoke a sense of awe. At the end of the worship service, having ignored all these animal spirits, we can still say that we have truly worshiped God in the Holy Spirit.

To be fair, modern worship leaders cannot be singled out for criticism. They are simply carrying on the long and regrettable tradition of church leaders who use images, pleasing sounds and shifting light to create fake feelings of the presence of God. Equally misguided are the 'smells and bells' worship services, or the powerful influence of late afternoon sunlight streaming through a stained glass window into a cathedral to the soaring accompaniment of a fine pipe organ.

None of these methods can bring us one inch closer to the Almighty. At best, they are completely unnecessary to worshiping God acceptably. At worst, they may even steal the undiscerning person away from true worship. As none of these stimulants matters to God in the least, we can be completely free from their influences.

Summary

It is good to be on the right road and continuing on a journey into worship that lines up biblically and with the best traditions of the worshiping church for the past 2,000 years. It is good to be freed from a dependence on man-made worship stimulants and free to worship God acceptably as he has so clearly taught us to do.

To God be the glory!

Chapter 20

Hymn-singer in a rock 'n' roll church:
tips for survival

Dear Dan,

I have read this far and it sounds great. I understand now what biblical worship is and what God expects of me as a worshiper. I'm glad I don't have to agree with every worship fad that comes along. It's really encouraging to know that I was not 'left behind' just because I still prefer a reverent service with great hymns of the faith.

But I'm stuck in a church that is changing to a modern worship format. We used to have a traditional service but that died out and now we have a so-called 'blended' service. I see all the problems you wrote about, but what can I do?

Should I stay or should I go? I don't want to leave because my friends are here and if I did, where would I go? It's not easy to find another good church in my town.

=============================

Unlike earlier letters in the book, this is not an actual letter from one reader. Here I tried to create a composite from the hundreds of letters I have received from people who feel stuck in churches that are headed down the wrong road of worship.

I suppose the easy thing to do would be to encourage these readers to leave that church and look for another. But I could never do that. God did not call me to a ministry of enticing members away from their church. After all, my work calls attention to errant worship practices that are doing just that, and I think it's a terrible thing to split churches over this.

To stay or to go because of worship problems must remain a personal and family decision. That decision has to be bathed in prayer and given time to consider. It is not something to be done hastily when feelings are running high. Many a Christian has left a church over the first offense without ever attempting to seek a peaceful resolution.

What else can a person do when they find themselves in this situation? I would like to share some practical tips for survival, based on many experiences with real people.

Make an appeal

We encourage readers to confront their church leaders in a gentle way. If you are uncomfortable with the changes, talk to your senior pastor as soon as possible and seek an audience to present your grievances.

If you are aware of others who are concerned, ask them to join you in the meeting with the pastor and let him know who you are bringing. The pastor may decide to invite others from 'his side' in response to that. But in the long run, the more people involved the better.

I can tell you from experience that the *wrong* way to confront the pastor is to slip copies of books like mine into his mailbox or hand one to him as you are leaving the service! I know many pastors personally. They are men much like other men, and will react defensively if you do that.

Some will attack the authors. I personally do not care what they say about me. God has surrounded me with many good men and women of God who pray for me and endorse my books, plus hundreds of thousands of readers who agree with me. I am more concerned with how this response may discourage you.

The best use of books like mine are as an example of someone who has articulated the same concerns you see, but which you may have found difficult to put into a statement to the pastor. I know how hard it is to confront a pastor. Most of us suffer from deep-seated feelings of inadequacy when it comes to discussing any spiritual matter with a leader, and here we are about to confront the man who is supposed to be the expert on all things related to church. Treat him with the honor and respect due his position, but don't be afraid to tell him what is on your conscience and always speak the truth in love.

If your church has a worship leader, I don't recommend that you speak to him or her first. The worship leader is a musician who is emotionally invested in the changes, putting all his passion and energy into it. He will be the least objective person in the church and may even be hurt that you are questioning the very thing he leads.

Keep in mind that he probably believes he is on a mission from God to help everyone worship in a better way. People on such a mission are inherently unable to see more than one side of a situation. Any criticism can be construed as personal, and that is not how you want to discuss your concerns.

Too many people try to win a debate on 'traditional v. modern worship' by presenting a stack of facts to the pastor. But most pastors are very good at oral arguments and know enough about the worship debate to easily disarm you.

That is why it is very important that you present your concerns first as a personal matter of conscience, instead of casting doubt on the motives of other Christians. Explain as best you can why a new (or perhaps old) worship practice is offensive to you, the concerns you have about its biblical basis, and how it will interfere with your ability to participate joyfully in the worship service.

Above all, pray for God to give you a winsome spirit. Few pastors can resist the power of an honest and sincere heart expressing a legitimate concern. If you run into the one who resists a sincere appeal, that man may not be fit to be a pastor and then your church has far more serious problems.

Some things never change

Many senior pastors believe they must change their worship practices and use modern worship innovations in order to attract visitors and to keep the young people in church. There is often a desperation behind this, as if this were the pastor's last chance to grow the church, and he may be inflexible as a result. How sad when a pastor stops trusting God for growth, turns instead to entertainment-driven worship as the new engine, and then refuses to listen to his own sheep.

If, after you have made your appeal in a respectful and biblical manner, the pastor informs you that he will not make any changes, you have a difficult decision to make. If you decide to stay at this church, be prepared to be marked as a troublemaker by the leaders — even if you are not. Your very presence at each service will be a witness against them, without a word being spoken.

You will need to decide how to deal with the service itself. Some people are strong enough to bear through it, while others are not and they cannot enjoy the rest of the service because of offensive music or dance or videos. If you are in the latter group, ask the pastor for permission to enter the service when the part that offends you has finished.

Many families have written about how they arrive in time for the offering and sermon, skipping the worship music and entertainment package, and slip quietly into a back row. In most churches, that will be noticed and there will be questions, so be ready to give an answer.

Start another service

You can also become a positive force for change. If your church has only one service and it has been turned into a combination of rock concert and late night talk show format, ask the pastor if the church will start a traditional service. Be prepared to discuss who you think would come and the volunteers you can line up to help with extra service tasks such as nursery and ushering.

You may be pleasantly surprised at some of the families who will show up at a traditional service. This is not only for the elderly; home-schooling families will be attracted, as well as some young married couples who were raised in a traditional setting. Even some of the most hard-core contemporary worship churches have 'rediscovered' traditional worship and started new services.

Summary

It is difficult to remain in a church when the style of worship changes and by conscience and biblical conviction you cannot support those changes. Sometimes the changes become offensive to the point where you can no longer worship in joy and peace.

Do your best to resolve this peacefully with the pastor. Do not become a gossip or the leader of a faction. If you have followed these steps, but there is no change in sight, and you cannot support the new style of worship, ask for one final meeting with the pastor. Inform him that if no changes can be made, then you can no longer worship at his church and would like to work together on a peaceful exit strategy.

Then will come the true test of Christian maturity for both parties. Pray for the peace of Christ.

Chapter 21

Take the tube to Elephant & Castle

You leave the United States on Saturday afternoon and fly into London's Heathrow airport, arriving early Sunday morning. Travel with a carry-on suitcase; you won't have time to wait for baggage. After you clear customs, stop in a restroom to change into a suit and tie, wash your face, comb your hair and brush your teeth. Men, you might need a shave too. There is enough time for a full English country breakfast at one of the arrival hall cafes; enjoy the baked beans and mushrooms but my advice is to skip the blood sausage.

After breakfast, head for the London Underground — Piccadilly Line; better known to locals as the tube. It's a short walk of a few hundred yards to the station, where you can buy a one-day travel card. Take the escalator down to the platform and catch the next train to London.

For the first several miles, you'll wonder why they call it the Underground as the train travels through residential neighborhoods above ground and on elevated rails. But soon the train heads downward and into the deep underground tunnels that criss-cross far beneath the streets of the ancient city of London. You're now underground in the tube.

On Sunday morning, tube travel is leisurely with a small number of fellow travelers and few, if any, delays. You should arrive at the Piccadilly Circus station about thirty minutes out of Heathrow. Exit the train and follow the signs to the Bakerloo Line. It's a brisk walk underground to make the transfer and you may need to carry your luggage up and down a few flights of stairs.

When you arrive at the Bakerloo Line, make sure to get on the southbound platform for the Elephant & Castle train. After a short trip of about ten minutes, exit the train at the end of the line: the Elephant & Castle stop. Climb the escalators and stairs to the west-side street exit, and walk outside. Look across the busy street and you see an impressive stone building with a classical portico dominated by Greek columns.

Gospel worship

You have arrived at Metropolitan Tabernacle, a Baptist church founded around 1650 and after 360 years still proclaiming the gospel of Jesus Christ to London. The church traces its roots to a congregation born at the same time Parliament issued a ban on Baptist meetings; that brave little group encountered constant persecution. The Tabernacle is located on a site thought to be where the Southwark Martyrs were burned at the stake. For this reason the foundation-stone of the church bears the words: 'The blood of the martyrs is the seed of the church.'

The Tabernacle is best known for its most famous preacher, Charles Haddon Spurgeon, who served as pastor from 1854 to 1892. During Spurgeon's ministry, tens of thousands were converted to God under the preaching of the Word.

Don't try to cross the road to the church. Americans fresh off the airplane in London tend to look the wrong way for oncoming traffic. You have come too far on the journey into worship for it to suddenly end right here. At any rate, there are barriers to discourage Americans from attempting it. Look for the pedestrian tunnel that takes you underneath the road and over to the other side.

The worship service begins at 11.00am and you are early, so you have time to chat with the greeters and look over the book tables filled with excellent literature. If this is your first time, ask to be seated in the balcony — first or second row — where you will have a birds-eye view of it all.

In reverence and awe

Before the service begins, the atmosphere inside the sanctuary is hushed and reverent. As the organist plays, people sit quietly in the pews — some in prayer, others deep in thought. You notice the racial diversity of the congregation, reflecting the multi-cultural population of London where it seems the Lord has brought people from all the nations to hear the gospel.

The pastor begins the service with a brief greeting and introduces the first hymn of the day. If you appreciate the sublime sacred hymns written by great English hymn-writers such as Watts, Wesley, Newton and Cowper, you are right at home. There is no song leader or 'worship' leader, per se; the accompanist sets the tune and tempo with a brief introduction and the congregation instinctively know when to start singing.

The singing is strong and you sense that people are paying close attention to the words. Every verse of the hymn is sung. Men sing the melody line, even the high notes, with enthusiasm and volume. This is strikingly different from American churches where the women typically sing the melody and men either sing parts, meekly sing the melody or do not sing at all.

The pastor prays a long and earnest pastoral prayer over the flock entrusted to him by the Lord Jesus. He prays for the sick and those confined to bed, for the local university students, for the nation of England to repent and experience revival, for the many missionaries supported by the church, for the persecuted Christians in many lands, and above all for the power of the gospel unto salvation for all who will hear it that day.

The Bible text for the sermon is read while the congregation follows along in their Bibles. There are one or two more hymns. Announcements are given but they are very brief and the tone is sober and appropriate to the occasion. There is no hint of entertainment or joking around. An offering is gathered after a prayer.

The sermon is expository, taken from the Bible text and explained by the pastor. He does not attempt to entertain the congregation. He permits the power of the words to have their way with the listeners. You sense how the Holy Spirit can work on hearts and minds all the better when he is not interrupted by human histrionics or rhetorical flourishes.

After the sermon, a closing hymn is sung, a prayer of benediction is offered, and the service is ended.

Come back this evening

There is a large banner outside the church advertising the evangelistic evening service. You are curious to see what changes and innovations will be made for that service, in order to 'be relevant to young people' and 'reach the unchurched'.

You return for the evangelistic service to find the Tabernacle packed with students from nearby universities. There are no attempts to cater to the students or the unsaved by using a rock band or a casually dressed preacher or videos or any other entertainment method. The order of service is the same as the morning service. The music is the same style and the atmosphere remains reverent.

What, then, makes this an *evangelistic* service? The only difference is this: the sermon is based on a Bible passage with a strong gospel message that can convict unbelievers of sin and show them the wonderful salvation in the name of the Lord.

End of the line

Business often takes me to London. I have been privileged to attend Metropolitan Tabernacle services on several occasions, and my wife Judi accompanied me once as well.

Here is what I have observed during my visits. The ministry of the Word is given primary place; a proper attitude of respect and reverence is sought after; the hymns contain some of the noblest lyrics ever written in the English language; the singing is accompanied by sacred music clearly separated from pop culture; and the Holy Spirit's work is not interfered with by the entertaining or charismatic powers of man.

Of course, the Tabernacle is not a perfect church; as the saying goes, there are no perfect churches because there are no perfect people. But did any of us really expect perfection? Of course not. Most of us will gladly settle for a church with a worship service similar to this, one that aspires to be:

- Biblical in everything done;
- Centered on the Word of God and the gospel;
- Filled with an attitude of reverence fit for meeting with God the Father and Jesus Christ the Son;
- Purposely seeking to be set apart from worldly affections;
- Purposely seeking to be anti-entertainment;
- Respectful of sacred traditions passed down to us;
- Filled with so much faith in the power of the gospel alone to save and sanctify that there is no need to embrace the worldly worship compromises of the church growth movement.

For me, Metropolitan Tabernacle and other churches around the world who follow a similar pattern symbolize the end of the line for my journey into worship. I have traveled a long way from a modern worship experience steeped in worldliness and pagan mysticism, informed by the entertainment values of a wicked world, and dependent on human performance and creativity to produce results. I thank God that he stripped away all of that, showed me the acts of worship that really matter to him, and gave me the peace and inner joy to be content with a simple gospel service.

I write this after my most recent visit in April 2010. May the Lord continue to preserve Metropolitan Tabernacle as an example of biblical, reverent, gospel worship.

Summary

Our journey into worship will not be finished until God calls us home some day, to join in the perfect worship around the throne in his presence. In the meantime, God has given us a roadmap guiding how to worship him while on earth and has left us examples from the saints who came before us. His worship is important enough that we should take the time to learn about it and conform our practices to it.

This book is a small attempt to bring attention to those simple directions, and to show Christians how to recognize wrong turns and dead-ends and get back on the right road. The ultimate goal is to glorify God.

However, none of this matters at all, if you are not a disciple of the Lord Jesus Christ. For God so loved you, that he gave his only begotten Son to die on the cross for you. If you repent of your sins, believe with your heart that God raised Jesus from the dead, and confess with your mouth that Jesus is the Lord, he will save you.

Saved from what? From God's eternal punishment in hell, which is the destiny for every sinner who rejects Jesus Christ. Now is the day of salvation; cry out to the Lord for mercy; do not put it off any longer, for none of us knows what the future holds.

Only when you become a Christian do you start the journey into worship. I hope and pray to see you soon, somewhere on that road.

As always, I welcome a respectful and honest dialogue with anyone who has comments or questions. Please write to me at danlucarini@msn.com. Every e-mail is answered in time.

May our great and gracious God grant us all repentance from worldliness and give us the will to reform our worship practices, so that they are pleasing and acceptable to him! Grace be with you.

Appendices

The complete list of Old Testament worship verses

(from the Authorized Version of the Holy Bible)

A list of 110 verses that contain one or more of the following words: worship, worships, worshiped, worshiping, worshiper, worshipers.

Genesis 22:5: And Abraham said unto his young men, Abide ye here with the ass; and I and the lad will go yonder and worship, and come again to you.

Genesis 24:26: And the man bowed down his head, and worshiped the LORD.

Genesis 24:48: And I bowed down my head, and worshiped the LORD, and blessed the LORD God of my master Abraham, which had led me in the right way to take my master's brother's daughter unto his son.

Genesis 24:52: And it came to pass, that, when Abraham's servant heard their words, he worshiped the LORD, bowing himself to the earth.

Exodus 4:31: And the people believed: and when they heard that the LORD had visited the children of Israel, and that he had looked upon their affliction, then they bowed their heads and worshiped.

Exodus 12:27: That ye shall say, It is the sacrifice of the LORD's passover, who passed over the houses of the children of Israel in Egypt, when he smote the Egyptians, and delivered our houses. And the people bowed the head and worshiped.

Exodus 24:1: And he said unto Moses, Come up unto the LORD, thou, and Aaron, Nadab, and Abihu, and seventy of the elders of Israel; and worship ye afar off.

Exodus 32:8: They have turned aside quickly out of the way which I commanded them: they have made them a molten calf, and have worshiped it, and have sacrificed thereunto, and said, These be thy gods, O Israel, which have brought thee up out of the land of Egypt.

Exodus 33:10: And all the people saw the cloudy pillar stand at the tabernacle door: and all the people rose up and worshiped, every man in his tent door.

Exodus 34:8: And Moses made haste, and bowed his head toward the earth, and worshiped.

Exodus 34:14: For thou shalt worship no other god: for the LORD, whose name is Jealous, is a jealous God.

Deuteronomy 4:19: And lest thou lift up thine eyes unto heaven, and when thou seest the sun, and the moon, and the stars, even all the host of heaven, shouldest be driven to worship them, and serve them, which the LORD thy God hath divided unto all nations under the whole heaven.

Deuteronomy 8:19: And it shall be, if thou do at all forget the LORD thy God, and walk after other gods, and serve them, and worship them, I testify against you this day that ye shall surely perish.

Deuteronomy 11:16: Take heed to yourselves, that your heart be not deceived, and ye turn aside, and serve other gods, and worship them.

Deuteronomy 17:3: And hath gone and served other gods, and worshiped them, either the sun, or moon, or any of the host of heaven, which I have not commanded.

Deuteronomy 26:10: And now, behold, I have brought the firstfruits of the land, which thou, O LORD, hast given me. And thou shalt set it before the LORD thy God, and worship before the LORD thy God.

Deuteronomy 29:26: For they went and served other gods, and worshiped them, gods whom they knew not, and whom he had not given unto them.

Deuteronomy 30:17: But if thine heart turn away, so that thou wilt not hear, but shalt be drawn away, and worship other gods, and serve them.

Joshua 5:14: And he said, Nay; but as captain of the host of the Lord am I now come. And Joshua fell on his face to the earth, and did worship, and said unto him, What saith my Lord unto his servant?

Judges 7:15: And it was so, when Gideon heard the telling of the dream, and the interpretation thereof, that he worshiped, and returned into the host of Israel, and said, Arise; for the Lord hath delivered into your hand the host of Midian.

1 Samuel 1:3: And this man went up out of his city yearly to worship and to sacrifice unto the Lord of hosts in Shiloh. And the two sons of Eli, Hophni and Phinehas, the priests of the Lord, were there.

1 Samuel 1:19: And they rose up in the morning early, and worshiped before the Lord, and returned, and came to their house to Ramah: and Elkanah knew Hannah his wife; and the Lord remembered her.

1 Samuel 1:28: Therefore also I have lent him to the Lord; as long as he liveth he shall be lent to the Lord. And he worshiped the Lord there.

1 Samuel 15:25: Now therefore, I pray thee, pardon my sin, and turn again with me, that I may worship the Lord.

1 Samuel 15:30: Then he said, I have sinned: yet honor me now, I pray thee, before the elders of my people, and before Israel, and turn again with me, that I may worship the Lord thy God.

1 Samuel 15:31: So Samuel turned again after Saul; and Saul worshiped the Lord.

2 Samuel 12:20: Then David arose from the earth, and washed, and anointed himself, and changed his apparel, and came into the house of the Lord, and worshiped: then he came to his own house; and when he required, they set bread before him, and he did eat.

2 Samuel 15:32: And it came to pass, that when David was come to the top of the mount, where he worshiped God, behold, Hushai the Archite came to meet him with his coat rent, and earth upon his head.

1 Kings 9:6: But if ye shall at all turn from following me, ye or your children, and will not keep my commandments and my statutes which I have set before you, but go and serve other gods, and worship them.

1 Kings 9:9: And they shall answer, Because they forsook the Lord their God, who brought forth their fathers out of the land of Egypt,

and have taken hold upon other gods, and have worshiped them, and served them: therefore hath the LORD brought upon them all this evil.

1 Kings 11:33: Because that they have forsaken me, and have worshiped Ashtoreth the goddess of the Zidonians, Chemosh the god of the Moabites, and Milcom the god of the children of Ammon, and have not walked in my ways, to do that which is right in mine eyes, and to keep my statutes and my judgments, as did David his father.

1 Kings 12:30: And this thing became a sin: for the people went to worship before the one, even unto Dan.

1 Kings 16:31: And it came to pass, as if it had been a light thing for him to walk in the sins of Jeroboam the son of Nebat, that he took to wife Jezebel the daughter of Ethbaal king of the Zidonians, and went and served Baal, and worshiped him.

1 Kings 22:53: For he served Baal, and worshiped him, and provoked to anger the LORD God of Israel, according to all that his father had done.

2 Kings 5:18: In this thing the LORD pardon thy servant, that when my master goeth into the house of Rimmon to worship there, and he leaneth on my hand, and I bow myself in the house of Rimmon: when I bow down myself in the house of Rimmon, the LORD pardon thy servant in this thing.

2 Kings 10:19: Now therefore call unto me all the prophets of Baal, all his servants, and all his priests; let none be wanting: for I have a great sacrifice to do to Baal; whosoever shall be wanting, he shall not live. But Jehu did it in subtilty, to the intent that he might destroy the worshipers of Baal.

2 Kings 10:21: And Jehu sent through all Israel: and all the worshipers of Baal came, so that there was not a man left that came not. And they came into the house of Baal; and the house of Baal was full from one end to another.

2 Kings 10:22: And he said unto him that was over the vestry, Bring forth vestments for all the worshipers of Baal. And he brought them forth vestments.

2 Kings 10:23: And Jehu went, and Jehonadab the son of Rechab, into the house of Baal, and said unto the worshipers of Baal, Search, and look that there be here with you none of the servants of the LORD, but the worshipers of Baal only.

2 Kings 17:16: And they left all the commandments of the Lord their God, and made them molten images, even two calves, and made a grove, and worshiped all the host of heaven, and served Baal.

2 Kings 17:36: But the Lord, who brought you up out of the land of Egypt with great power and a stretched out arm, him shall ye fear, and him shall ye worship, and to him shall ye do sacrifice.

2 Kings 18:22: But if ye say unto me, We trust in the Lord our God: is not that he, whose high places and whose altars Hezekiah hath taken away, and hath said to Judah and Jerusalem, Ye shall worship before this altar in Jerusalem?

2 Kings 19:37: And it came to pass, as he was worshiping in the house of Nisroch his god, that Adrammelech and Sharezer his sons smote him with the sword: and they escaped into the land of Armenia. And Esarhaddon his son reigned in his stead.

2 Kings 21:3: For he built up again the high places which Hezekiah his father had destroyed; and he reared up altars for Baal, and made a grove, as did Ahab king of Israel; and worshiped all the host of heaven, and served them.

2 Kings 21:21: And he walked in all the way that his father walked in, and served the idols that his father served, and worshiped them.

1 Chronicles 16:29: Give unto the Lord the glory due unto his name: bring an offering, and come before him: worship the Lord in the beauty of holiness.

1 Chronicles 29:20: And David said to all the congregation, Now bless the Lord your God. And all the congregation blessed the Lord God of their fathers, and bowed down their heads, and worshiped the Lord, and the king.

2 Chronicles 7:3: And when all the children of Israel saw how the fire came down, and the glory of the Lord upon the house, they bowed themselves with their faces to the ground upon the pavement, and worshiped, and praised the Lord, saying, For he is good; for his mercy endureth for ever.

2 Chronicles 7:19: But if ye turn away, and forsake my statutes and my commandments, which I have set before you, and shall go and serve other gods, and worship them.

2 Chronicles 7:22: And it shall be answered, Because they forsook the Lord God of their fathers, which brought them forth out of the land of Egypt, and laid hold on other gods, and worshiped them,

and served them: therefore hath he brought all this evil upon them.

2 Chronicles 20:18: And Jehoshaphat bowed his head with his face to the ground: and all Judah and the inhabitants of Jerusalem fell before the LORD, worshiping the LORD.

2 Chronicles 29:28: And all the congregation worshiped, and the singers sang, and the trumpeters sounded: and all this continued until the burnt offering was finished.

2 Chronicles 29:29: And when they had made an end of offering, the king and all that were present with him bowed themselves, and worshiped.

2 Chronicles 29:30: Moreover Hezekiah the king and the princes commanded the Levites to sing praise unto the LORD with the words of David, and of Asaph the seer. And they sang praises with gladness, and they bowed their heads and worshiped.

2 Chronicles 32:12: Hath not the same Hezekiah taken away his high places and his altars, and commanded Judah and Jerusalem, saying, Ye shall worship before one altar, and burn incense upon it?

2 Chronicles 33:3: For he built again the high places which Hezekiah his father had broken down, and he reared up altars for Baalim, and made groves, and worshiped all the host of heaven, and served them.

Nehemiah 8:6: And Ezra blessed the LORD, the great God. And all the people answered, Amen, Amen, with lifting up their hands: and they bowed their heads, and worshiped the LORD with their faces to the ground.

Nehemiah 9:3: And they stood up in their place, and read in the book of the law of the LORD their God one fourth part of the day; and another fourth part they confessed, and worshiped the LORD their God.

Job 1:20: Then Job arose, and rent his mantle, and shaved his head, and fell down upon the ground, and worshiped.

Psalm 5:7: But as for me, I will come into thy house in the multitude of thy mercy: and in thy fear will I worship toward thy holy temple.

Psalm 22:27: All the ends of the world shall remember and turn unto the LORD: and all the kindreds of the nations shall worship before thee.

Psalm 22:29: All they that be fat upon earth shall eat and worship: all they that go down to the dust shall bow before him: and none can keep alive his own soul.

Psalm 29:2: Give unto the LORD the glory due unto his name; worship the LORD in the beauty of holiness.

Psalm 45:11: So shall the king greatly desire thy beauty: for he is thy Lord; and worship thou him.

Psalm 66:4: All the earth shall worship thee, and shall sing unto thee; they shall sing to thy name. Selah.

Psalm 81:9: There shall no strange god be in thee; neither shalt thou worship any strange god.

Psalm 86:9: All nations whom thou hast made shall come and worship before thee, O Lord; and shall glorify thy name.

Psalm 95:6: O come, let us worship and bow down: let us kneel before the LORD our maker.

Psalm 96:9: O worship the LORD in the beauty of holiness: fear before him, all the earth.

Psalm 97:7: Confounded be all they that serve graven images, that boast themselves of idols: worship him, all ye gods.

Psalm 99:5: Exalt ye the LORD our God, and worship at his footstool; for he is holy.

Psalm 99:9: Exalt the LORD our God, and worship at his holy hill; for the LORD our God is holy.

Psalm 106:19: They made a calf in Horeb, and worshiped the molten image.

Psalm 132:7: We will go into his tabernacles: we will worship at his footstool.

Psalm 138:2: I will worship toward thy holy temple, and praise thy name for thy lovingkindness and for thy truth: for thou hast magnified thy word above all thy name.

Isaiah 2:8: Their land also is full of idols; they worship the work of their own hands, that which their own fingers have made.

Isaiah 2:20: In that day a man shall cast his idols of silver, and his idols of gold, which they made each one for himself to worship, to the moles and to the bats.

Isaiah 27:13: And it shall come to pass in that day, that the great trumpet shall be blown, and they shall come which were ready to perish in the land of Assyria, and the outcasts in the land of Egypt, and shall worship the LORD in the holy mount at Jerusalem.

Isaiah 36:7: But if thou say to me, We trust in the LORD our God: is it not he, whose high places and whose altars Hezekiah hath taken away, and said to Judah and to Jerusalem, Ye shall worship before this altar?

Isaiah 37:38: And it came to pass, as he was worshiping in the house of Nisroch his god, that Adrammelech and Sharezer his sons smote him with the sword; and they escaped into the land of Armenia: and Esarhaddon his son reigned in his stead.

Isaiah 46:6: They lavish gold out of the bag, and weigh silver in the balance, and hire a goldsmith; and he maketh it a god: they fall down, yea, they worship.

Isaiah 49:7: Thus saith the LORD, the Redeemer of Israel, and his Holy One, to him whom man despiseth, to him whom the nation abhorreth, to a servant of rulers, Kings shall see and arise, princes also shall worship, because of the LORD that is faithful, and the Holy One of Israel, and he shall choose thee.

Isaiah 66:23: And it shall come to pass, that from one new moon to another, and from one sabbath to another, shall all flesh come to worship before me, saith the LORD.

Jeremiah 1:16: And I will utter my judgments against them touching all their wickedness, who have forsaken me, and have burned incense unto other gods, and worshiped the works of their own hands.

Jeremiah 7:2: Stand in the gate of the LORD's house, and proclaim there this word, and say, Hear the word of the LORD, all ye of Judah, that enter in at these gates to worship the LORD.

Jeremiah 8:2: And they shall spread them before the sun, and the moon, and all the host of heaven, whom they have loved, and whom they have served, and after whom they have walked, and whom they have sought, and whom they have worshiped: they shall not be gathered, nor be buried; they shall be for dung upon the face of the earth.

Jeremiah 13:10: This evil people, which refuse to hear my words, which walk in the imagination of their heart, and walk after other gods, to serve them, and to worship them, shall even be as this girdle, which is good for nothing.

Jeremiah 16:11: Then shalt thou say unto them, Because your fathers have forsaken me, saith the LORD, and have walked after other gods, and have served them, and have worshiped them, and have forsaken me, and have not kept my law.

Jeremiah 22:9: Then they shall answer, Because they have forsaken the covenant of the LORD their God, and worshiped other gods, and served them.

Jeremiah 25:6: And go not after other gods to serve them, and to worship them, and provoke me not to anger with the works of your hands; and I will do you no hurt.

Jeremiah 26:2: Thus saith the LORD; Stand in the court of the LORD's house, and speak unto all the cities of Judah, which come to worship in the LORD's house, all the words that I command thee to speak unto them; diminish not a word.

Jeremiah 44:19: And when we burned incense to the queen of heaven, and poured out drink offerings unto her, did we make her cakes to worship her, and pour out drink offerings unto her, without our men?

Ezekiel 8:16: And he brought me into the inner court of the LORD's house, and, behold, at the door of the temple of the LORD, between the porch and the altar, were about five and twenty men, with their backs toward the temple of the LORD, and their faces toward the east; and they worshiped the sun toward the east.

Ezekiel 46:2: And the prince shall enter by the way of the porch of that gate without, and shall stand by the post of the gate, and the priests shall prepare his burnt offering and his peace offerings, and he shall worship at the threshold of the gate: then he shall go forth; but the gate shall not be shut until the evening.

Ezekiel 46:3: Likewise the people of the land shall worship at the door of this gate before the LORD in the sabbaths and in the new moons.

Ezekiel 46:9: But when the people of the land shall come before the LORD in the solemn feasts, he that entereth in by the way of the north gate to worship shall go out by the way of the south gate; and he that entereth by the way of the south gate shall go forth by the way of the north gate: he shall not return by the way of the gate whereby he came in, but shall go forth over against it.

Daniel 2:46: Then the king Nebuchadnezzar fell upon his face, and worshiped Daniel, and commanded that they should offer an oblation and sweet odours unto him.

Daniel 3:5: That at what time ye hear the sound of the cornet, flute, harp, sackbut, psaltery, dulcimer, and all kinds of musick, ye fall down and worship the golden image that Nebuchadnezzar the king hath set up.

Daniel 3:7: Therefore at that time, when all the people heard the sound of the cornet, flute, harp, sackbut, psaltery, and all kinds of musick, all the people, the nations, and the languages, fell down and worshiped the golden image that Nebuchadnezzar the king had set up.

Daniel 3:10: Thou, O king, hast made a decree, that every man that shall hear the sound of the cornet, flute, harp, sackbut, psaltery, and dulcimer, and all kinds of musick, shall fall down and worship the golden image.

Daniel 3:12: There are certain Jews whom thou hast set over the affairs of the province of Babylon, Shadrach, Meshach, and Abednego; these men, O king, have not regarded thee: they serve not thy gods, nor worship the golden image which thou hast set up.

Daniel 3:14: Nebuchadnezzar spake and said unto them, Is it true, O Shadrach, Meshach, and Abednego, do not ye serve my gods, nor worship the golden image which I have set up?

Daniel 3:15: Now if ye be ready that at what time ye hear the sound of the cornet, flute, harp, sackbut, psaltery, and dulcimer, and all kinds of musick, ye fall down and worship the image which I have made; well: but if ye worship not, ye shall be cast the same hour into the midst of a burning fiery furnace; and who is that God that shall deliver you out of my hands?

Daniel 3:18: But if not, be it known unto thee, O king, that we will not serve thy gods, nor worship the golden image which thou hast set up.

Daniel 3:28: Then Nebuchadnezzar spake, and said, Blessed be the God of Shadrach, Meshach, and Abednego, who hath sent his angel, and delivered his servants that trusted in him, and have changed the king's word, and yielded their bodies, that they might not serve nor worship any god, except their own God.

Micah 5:13: Thy graven images also will I cut off, and thy standing images out of the midst of thee; and thou shalt no more worship the work of thine hands.

Zephaniah 1:5: And them that worship the host of heaven upon the housetops; and them that worship and that swear by the LORD, and that swear by Malcham.

Zephaniah 2:11: The LORD will be terrible unto them: for he will famish all the gods of the earth; and men shall worship him, every one from his place, even all the isles of the heathen.

Zechariah 14:16: And it shall come to pass, that every one that is left of all the nations which came against Jerusalem shall even go up from year to year to worship the King, the LORD of hosts, and to keep the feast of tabernacles.

Zechariah 14:17: And it shall be, that whoso will not come up of all the families of the earth unto Jerusalem to worship the King, the LORD of hosts, even upon them shall be no rain.

Appendix B

The complete list of New Testament

worship verses

(from the Authorized Version of the Holy Bible)

A list of 72 verses that contain one or more of the following words:
worship, worships, worshiped, worshiping, worshiper, worshipers.

Matthew 2:2: Saying, Where is he that is born King of the Jews? for we have seen his star in the east, and are come to worship him.

Matthew 2:8: And he sent them to Bethlehem, and said, Go and search diligently for the young child; and when ye have found him, bring me word again, that I may come and worship him also.

Matthew 2:11: And when they were come into the house, they saw the young child with Mary his mother, and fell down, and worshiped him: and when they had opened their treasures, they presented unto him gifts; gold, and frankincense, and myrrh.

Matthew 4:9: And saith unto him, All these things will I give thee, if thou wilt fall down and worship me.

Matthew 4:10: Then saith Jesus unto him, Get thee hence, Satan: for it is written, Thou shalt worship the Lord thy God, and him only shalt thou serve.

Matthew 8:2: And, behold, there came a leper and worshiped him, saying, Lord, if thou wilt, thou canst make me clean.

Matthew 9:18: While he spake these things unto them, behold, there came a certain ruler, and worshiped him, saying, My daughter is even now dead: but come and lay thy hand upon her, and she shall live.

Matthew 14:33: Then they that were in the ship came and worshiped him, saying, Of a truth thou art the Son of God.

Matthew 15:9: But in vain they do worship me, teaching for doctrines the commandments of men.

Matthew 15:25: Then came she and worshiped him, saying, Lord, help me.

Matthew 18:26: The servant therefore fell down, and worshiped him, saying, Lord, have patience with me, and I will pay thee all.

Matthew 20:20: Then came to him the mother of Zebedee's children with her sons, worshiping him, and desiring a certain thing of him.

Matthew 28:9: And as they went to tell his disciples, behold, Jesus met them, saying, All hail. And they came and held him by the feet, and worshiped him.

Matthew 28:17: And when they saw him, they worshiped him: but some doubted.

Mark 5:6: But when he saw Jesus afar off, he ran and worshiped him.

Mark 7:7: Howbeit in vain do they worship me, teaching for doctrines the commandments of men.

Mark 15:19: And they smote him on the head with a reed, and did spit upon him, and bowing their knees worshiped him.

Luke 4:7: If thou therefore wilt worship me, all shall be thine.

Luke 4:8: And Jesus answered and said unto him, Get thee behind me, Satan: for it is written, Thou shalt worship the Lord thy God, and him only shalt thou serve.

Luke 14:10: But when thou art bidden, go and sit down in the lowest room; that when he that bade thee cometh, he may say unto thee, Friend, go up higher: then shalt thou have worship in the presence of them that sit at meat with thee.

Luke 24:52: And they worshiped him, and returned to Jerusalem with great joy.

John 4:20: Our fathers worshiped in this mountain; and ye say, that in Jerusalem is the place where men ought to worship.

John 4:21: Jesus saith unto her, Woman, believe me, the hour cometh, when ye shall neither in this mountain, nor yet at Jerusalem, worship the Father.

John 4:22: Ye worship ye know not what: we know what we worship: for salvation is of the Jews.

John 4:23: But the hour cometh, and now is, when the true worshipers shall worship the Father in spirit and in truth: for the Father seeketh such to worship him.

John 4:24: God is a Spirit: and they that worship him must worship him in spirit and in truth.

John 9:31: Now we know that God heareth not sinners: but if any man be a worshiper of God, and doeth his will, him he heareth.

John 9:38: And he said, Lord, I believe. And he worshiped him.

John 12:20: And there were certain Greeks among them that came up to worship at the feast.

Acts 7:42: Then God turned, and gave them up to worship the host of heaven; as it is written in the book of the prophets, O ye house of Israel, have ye offered to me slain beasts and sacrifices by the space of forty years in the wilderness?

Acts 7:43: Yea, ye took up the tabernacle of Moloch, and the star of your god Remphan, figures which ye made to worship them: and I will carry you away beyond Babylon.

Acts 8:27: And he arose and went: and, behold, a man of Ethiopia, an eunuch of great authority under Candace queen of the Ethiopians, who had the charge of all her treasure, and had come to Jerusalem for to worship,

Acts 10:25: And as Peter was coming in, Cornelius met him, and fell down at his feet, and worshiped him.

Acts 16:14: And a certain woman named Lydia, a seller of purple, of the city of Thyatira, which worshiped God, heard us: whose heart the Lord opened, that she attended unto the things which were spoken of Paul.

Acts 17:23: For as I passed by, and beheld your devotions, I found an altar with this inscription, TO THE UNKNOWN GOD. Whom therefore ye ignorantly worship, him declare I unto you.

Acts 17:25: Neither is worshiped with men's hands, as though he needed any thing, seeing he giveth to all life, and breath, and all things.

Acts 18:7: And he departed thence, and entered into a certain man's house, named Justus, one that worshiped God, whose house joined hard to the synagogue.

Acts 18:13: Saying, This fellow persuadeth men to worship God contrary to the law.

Acts 19:35: And when the townclerk had appeased the people, he said, Ye men of Ephesus, what man is there that knoweth not how that the city of the Ephesians is a worshiper of the great goddess Diana, and of the image which fell down from Jupiter? [a worshiper: Gr. the temple keeper]

Acts 24:11: Because that thou mayest understand, that there are yet but twelve days since I went up to Jerusalem for to worship.

Acts 24:14: But this I confess unto thee, that after the way which they call heresy, so worship I the God of my fathers, believing all things which are written in the law and in the prophets.

Romans 1:25: Who changed the truth of God into a lie, and worshiped and served the creature more than the Creator, who is blessed for ever. Amen.

1 Corinthians 14:25: And thus are the secrets of his heart made manifest; and so falling down on his face he will worship God, and report that God is in you of a truth.

Philippians 3:3: For we are the circumcision, which worship God in the spirit, and rejoice in Christ Jesus, and have no confidence in the flesh.

Colossians 2:18: Let no man beguile you of your reward in a voluntary humility and worshiping of angels, intruding into those things which he hath not seen, vainly puffed up by his fleshly mind.

Colossians 2:23: Which things have indeed a shew of wisdom in will worship, and humility, and neglecting of the body; not in any honour to the satisfying of the flesh.

2 Thessalonians 2:4: Who opposeth and exalteth himself above all that is called God, or that is worshiped; so that he as God sitteth in the temple of God, shewing himself that he is God.

Hebrews 1:6: And again, when he bringeth in the firstbegotten into the world, he saith, And let all the angels of God worship him.

Hebrews 10:2: For then would they not have ceased to be offered? because that the worshipers once purged should have had no more conscience of sins.

Hebrews 11:21: By faith Jacob, when he was a dying, blessed both the sons of Joseph; and worshiped, leaning upon the top of his staff.

Revelation 3:9: Behold, I will make them of the synagogue of Satan, which say they are Jews, and are not, but do lie; behold, I will make them to come and worship before thy feet, and to know that I have loved thee.

Revelation 4:10: The four and twenty elders fall down before him that sat on the throne, and worship him that liveth for ever and ever, and cast their crowns before the throne, saying...

Revelation 5:14: And the four beasts said, Amen. And the four and twenty elders fell down and worshiped him that liveth for ever and ever.

Revelation 7:11: And all the angels stood round about the throne, and about the elders and the four beasts, and fell before the throne on their faces, and worshiped God.

Revelation 9:20: And the rest of the men which were not killed by these plagues yet repented not of the works of their hands, that they should not worship devils, and idols of gold, and silver, and brass, and stone, and of wood: which neither can see, nor hear, nor walk.

Revelation 11:1: And there was given me a reed like unto a rod: and the angel stood, saying, Rise, and measure the temple of God, and the altar, and them that worship therein.

Revelation 11:16: And the four and twenty elders, which sat before God on their seats, fell upon their faces, and worshiped God.

Revelation 13:4: And they worshiped the dragon which gave power unto the beast: and they worshiped the beast, saying, Who is like unto the beast? who is able to make war with him?

Revelation 13:8: And all that dwell upon the earth shall worship him, whose names are not written in the book of life of the Lamb slain from the foundation of the world.

Revelation 13:12: And he exerciseth all the power of the first beast before him, and causeth the earth and them which dwell therein to worship the first beast, whose deadly wound was healed.

Revelation 13:15: And he had power to give life unto the image of the beast, that the image of the beast should both speak, and cause that as many as would not worship the image of the beast should be killed.

Revelation 14:7: Saying with a loud voice, Fear God, and give glory to him; for the hour of his judgment is come: and worship him that made heaven, and earth, and the sea, and the fountains of waters.

Revelation 14:9: And the third angel followed them, saying with a loud voice, If any man worship the beast and his image, and receive his mark in his forehead, or in his hand,

Revelation 14:11: And the smoke of their torment ascendeth up for ever and ever: and they have no rest day nor night, who worship the beast and his image, and whosoever receiveth the mark of his name.

Revelation 15:4: Who shall not fear thee, O Lord, and glorify thy name? for thou only art holy: for all nations shall come and worship before thee; for thy judgments are made manifest.

Revelation 16:2: And the first went, and poured out his vial upon the earth; and there fell a noisome and grievous sore upon the men which had the mark of the beast, and upon them which worshiped his image.

Revelation 19:4: And the four and twenty elders and the four beasts fell down and worshiped God that sat on the throne, saying, Amen; Alleluia.

Revelation 19:10: And I fell at his feet to worship him. And he said unto me, See thou do it not: I am thy fellowservant, and of thy brethren that have the testimony of Jesus: worship God: for the testimony of Jesus is the spirit of prophecy.

Revelation 19:20: And the beast was taken, and with him the false prophet that wrought miracles before him, with which he deceived them that had received the mark of the beast, and them that worshiped his image. These both were cast alive into a lake of fire burning with brimstone.

Revelation 20:4: And I saw thrones, and they sat upon them, and judgment was given unto them: and I saw the souls of them that were beheaded for the witness of Jesus, and for the word of God, and which had not worshiped the beast, neither his image, neither had received his mark upon their foreheads, or in their hands; and they lived and reigned with Christ a thousand years.

Revelation 22:8: And I John saw these things, and heard them. And when I had heard and seen, I fell down to worship before the feet of the angel which shewed me these things.

Revelation 22:9: Then saith he unto me, See thou do it not: for I am thy fellowservant, and of thy brethren the prophets, and of them which keep the sayings of this book: worship God.

Guidelines for choosing music
for the church

This is my attempt at a decision grid for evaluating music styles for worship — using spiritual principles instead of music criteria.

Biblical guideline	Scripture reference	Examine the music style
1. Use spiritual songs.	Ephesians 5:19; Colossians 3:16	Appeals first and mainly to the spirit or the flesh?
2. Live pure and holy lives.	Romans 12:1-2; 1 Corinthians 6:18; Ephesians 5:3; 1 Thessalonians 4:1-7	Associated with purity or with fornication? Does it control my body?
3. Don't love the things of the world: lust of the eyes, lust of the flesh, pride of life.	1 John 2:15-17	Does it promote any of these 'things of the world'?

Biblical guideline	Scripture reference	Examine the music style
4. Don't have fellowship with demons.	1 Corinthians 10:18-22; Acts 15:20	Connected in any way with demons? The rhythms?
5. Honor your father and mother. Respect those over you in the Lord.	Exodus 20:12; Ephesians 6:2; 1 Thessalonians 5:12	Respectful to parents & grandparents? Or the music of rebels?
6. Flee from idolatry.	Exodus 20:4-5; 1 Corinthians 10:14; Acts 15:20; 2 Corinthians 6:14-16	Used to serve today's idols, or clearly separated?
7. Have a meek and quiet spirit, and live peacefully.	1 Timothy 2:2; 1 Peter 3:4; Galatians 5:22	Is it loud, party music?
8. Don't cause a brother to stumble and fall.	Romans 14:13	Think first — who would it harm or disturb if I used it?

Other books from the author...

Also translated into Russian

Why I left the Contemporary Christian Music Movement

'Dan Lucarini invites us to wrestle with a major issue perplexing churches all over the world today. His diagnosis and prescription is going to anger some, not because of his tone (he is charitable, but firm throughout) but because he is touching a very sensitive nerve in the modern evangelical church. The matters he raises are all real and the cautions he brings are surely timely. If you consider yourself "traditional" in your approach to worship and music in the church, Lucarini provides you with an outline of almost all the key matters that must be addressed in the church's assessment of the usefulness of new musical forms. If you consider yourself "contemporary" in your perspective on worship, Lucarini raises the questions that you need to provide a sound biblical answer to before committing the church to a new direction in its corporate praise.'

J. Ligon Duncan III, PhD
Minister, First Presbyterian Church, Jackson, Mississippi, USA
Adjunct Professor, Reformed Theological Seminary
Council, Alliance of Confessing Evangelicals

'The author's honest sharing of his own spiritual and musical journey prepares the way for his assessment of what he sees to be a major problem in today's church... Lucarini's direct and uncompromising style is harnessed to a gracious spirit concerned with nothing else but God's glory. This is nowhere more evident than in his warm and wise treatment of the subject of worship and ministry.'

John Blanchard

EP Books, 144 pages. ISBN-13: 978-0-85234-517-7.

Can we
rock
the gospel?

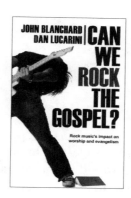

by John Blanchard and Dan Lucarini

Few subjects generate more heat in the Christian church today than the use of music in worship and evangelism. Every musical form and every way of expressing it has as many detractors as it does promoters. Yet in recent years most of the conflicts have centered on what is generically known as rock music, which has become an increasingly dominant — and divisive — issue since it first slipped into church life some forty years ago.

For some Christians it is by far the best way of expressing their faith and of sharing it with unbelievers, while for other Christians it is by far the worst. Does the truth lie somewhere between these two extremes? Does God endorse music of every kind? Can we 'cut and paste' secular rock music and 'Christianize' it in the process? Should the Christian church unite in bringing rock music to the altar or in sending it to the bonfire?

Two respected Christian leaders and best-selling authors who together have many years of hands-on experience in worship, preaching, evangelism and music have combined to produce a book that examines this controversial subject, using both recent evidence and time-tested truths.

They come to a clear conclusion. They will not leave you neutral.

EP Books, 272 pages. ISBN-13: 978-0-85234-628-0.

A wide range of Christian books is available from EP Books. If you would like a free catalogue please write to us or contact us by e-mail. Alternatively, you can view the whole catalogue online at our web site:

www.epbooks.org

EP BOOKS
Faverdale North, Darlington, DL3 0PH, England

e-mail: sales@epbooks.org

EP BOOKS USA
P. O. Box 614, Carlisle, PA 17013, USA

www.epbooks.us

e-mail: usasales@epbooks.org